Chapter 1

Introduction to Python

1.1 What is python?

Python is extensively used general purpose, high level popular programming language created by *Guido van Rossum* in 1991. As per Github's octoverse, Python is the second most used language by developers in 2019.

Python is one of the most popular languages in 21th century because it is so productive compare to other programming languages. It is easy to read, code or to understand because of its simple syntax.

1.1.1 Why we need it?

We need a programming language to write any kind of software. Without software it is not possible to run hard components.

1.1.1.1 Software

Software is a program or set of programs written by using programming languages.

- Software is responsible for running hardware.
- All operating systems are also software.
- Operating system controls and runs all hardware.

1.2 Beginning with Python programming

Before we start a Python Programming we must know what are basically **Complier and Interpreted**

When we write a code we know that it is executes with the help of the back-end system. This checking system is whether Interpreted or a Complier.

1.2.1 Complier

- It translates the whole programme given to it into machine code (1's and 0's).
- It takes large amount of time to analyse the high level code but the overall execution time is completely faster.
- As it requires more memory than interpreter because it generates intermediate object code which further requires linking.
- It generates the error message only after scanning the whole programme so debugging is comparatively hard.
- Programming language like C, C++, Swift, Erlang uses compilers.

1.2.2 Interpreter

- It translates one by one line of the whole programme into machine code.

- It takes less amount of time to analyse the high level code (given by programmer also called source code) but the overall execution time is slower.
- As they are memory efficient because no intermediate object code is generated in it.
- It continues translating the programme until the first error is met, in that case it stops. So debugging is easy as we can find the bug easily.
- Programming language like **Python**, Ruby, Perl, PHP use Interpreters.

1.2.3 Python reserved words

Python have some reserved words also called **keywords.** They are special words acts as a programming instruction, defined with predefined meaning and syntax in the language. We cannot use them for variable or function. If you use any of them as a variable name it makes a syntax error so you should kept this thing in your mind that error may be generated because you are using one of these words.

and	finally	None
as	false	not
assert	for	or

break	from	pass
class	global	raise
continue	if	return
def	import	True
del	In	try
elif	Is	with
else	lambda	while
except	nonlocal	yield

Remember: As python is case-sensitive .The keyword **and** cannot written as **And** or **True** as **true.**

Chapter 2

Print

The print function in Python prints all the given statement inside the parentheses to the output console window. These input statements can be Integers, Strings or Float. This function is most widely used in the programs.

2.1 Integer

Integer is a whole number. To print that, we do not use quotation marks. We can write the code as follows,

```
print(123)
```

123

2.2 String

We can print any string value as following,

```
print('Python for the beginners')
```

Python for the beginners

> **Remember**: To print text, which is also called string, we use quotation marks. Without using quotation marks, it makes an error.

Here we print the sting without quotes,

```
print(Python for the beginners)
```

```
  File "<ipython-input-2-32104f401b95>", line 1
    print(Python for the beginners)
                        ^
SyntaxError: invalid syntax
```

Note: Whatever inside quotation marks is treated like a string whether it is a text, integer or a float.

```
print('123')
```

123

As **123** is integer but here it is written inside quotation ("") so it is not integer anymore but become a string.

2.3 Float

The whole number with the decimal point called float value. Like in Integer, quotation mark is not essential but quotation marks treated it like string value.

```
print('9.9')
```

9.9

Remember: The function **print** takes one or more than one input and prints as it is to the screen. Values separated by comma. Comma tells Interpreter that new value starts.

We can see in the following block of code that there is space between the outputs as print function have default separator **space**. Separator tells us how two values will be separate.

```
print("Hello",123,345,13.2)
```
```
Hello 123 345 13.2
```

💡 **Hint:** You can see signature of any function by putting cursor inside parentheses and pressing "Shift"+ "Tab". Signature tells us that the function takes which type of input. In the following block we see the signature of function **print ()**

```
print()
```
```
Docstring:                                    ^ + ✕
print(value, ...,          , end='\n', file=sys.stdout, flush=False)

Prints the values to a stream, or to sys.stdout by default.
```

💡 **Knowledge:** You can change default separator by any value you want like,

```
print("Hello",123,345,13.2,sep="-----")
```
```
Hello-----123-----345-----13.2
```

Task: 1) Change default value of end to any other value.

(Hint: To see its effect use multiple print () functions)

2) "\n" is Escape character .Explore more escape character to learn more.

7

Chapter 3

Variable

As the name implies, a variable is something that can change/Variable or not consistent. It can change with the time. In simplest terms, a variable is just a box that you can putt stuff in, but see you can put more stuff in the similar box or take some out.

A variable in python is a **placeholder** that holds a value that may change. Variable can store all kind of stuff whether it is a string, float or a number.

3.1 Rules for naming a variable

1. Variable can't enclose in quotation marks like "number"=1.

2. Variable can't have any spaces in it. If you want to use more than one word as a variable, you can use underscore which helps us easy to read like **my_lucky_number=1.**

3. It can't be python reserved name discussed in chapter 1.

4. It can't be a number or begin with a number like 123=456.

```
1st_day="Monday"
```

```
  File "<ipython-input-53-8b962dcf325e>", line 1
    1st_day="Monday"
           ^
SyntaxError: invalid syntax
```

But this does not make error because 1 comes later in the variable name as follows

```
Day_1="Monday"
```

```
print(Day_1)
```

```
Monday
```

So Python variables can also change like this.

3.2 Storing string in a variable:

Whenever we store a value in a variable it store in the memory and whenever we need it we call for the variable where it is store. For example someone says,

"My name is Laura and I am in 6th grade"

You just memorized that a girl name **Laura** is in grade 6th but after 1 year, when she passed the exam and moved to 7th Grade. If she wants you to know her grade, she'll to tell you that she is now in 7th grade. After she tell you, you'll know that Laura's grade doesn't refer to the original value,"6th ", but now refers to a new value, "7th".

Let's do an example. Here we store the *Linna* is variable *Name* and execute it.

```
Name="Linna"
```

```
Name
```
```
'Linna'
```

Also, we can print a string with the variable like,

```
print("Hi!"+Name)
```
```
Hi!Linna
```

```
type(Name)
```
```
str
```

Task: Assign a string to a variable. You can name the variable and the string as you want. Using the variable, write a statement that displays the string on the console.

The output shows that variable **Name** store string value i-e **Linna**

 **Knowledge**: Initially variables have no data type unless we give the value to the variable .We check data type of any variable by function **type ()**.

3.2.1 Concatenate

Concatenate means appending one string to another string. It is done by using '**+**' operator between them.

```
first_name="linna"
last_name="Buran"
```

```
print(first_name+last_name)
```

```
linnaBuran
```

Remember: In string, **+** operator is not for addition but concatenate.

Here we can see that value **12** and **34** is assign to the variables **num1** and **num2** as follows,

```
num1="12"
num2="34"
```

We concatenate these variables to the new variable *result.* One thing to be noted that it would not work, the result might be *1234* rather than *46* as Python can't sum strings. We can see the output as follows,

```
result=num1+num2
```

```
print(result)
```
```
1234
```

Task: Try to sum a string and the integer

(Hint: Assign string and variable to separate variables add them)

 Key:

- "=" sign in python called **assignment variable.**
- A variable name also called **identifier**.

3.3 Storing float in a variable

We can store any float value in the variable. In the following, we define a variable *decimal* and assign float value *9.8* to it

```
decimal=9.8
```

When we call variable *decimal* we get the following output,

```
print(decimal)
```
```
9.8
```

3.3.1 Adding value to the variable

We can use the existing variable and add values to it. Here we add integer value *1* to the *decimal*. i-e 9.8 + 1 equals to 10.8,

```
print(decimal + 1)
```
10.8

Similarly, we can also add float to the variable *decimal* as follows,

```
print(decimal + 2.1)
```
11.9

3.4 Storing integer in a variable

In the following, integer value *1* is assign to a variable *x,*

```
x=1
```

Whenever you have to access value 1 you pass variable to the **print** function as follows,

```
print(x)
```
1

3.4.1 Overwrite

If we assign new value to the same variable it removes the previous values and store new value. Here it prints *1.1* rather than *1*.

```
x=1.1
```

```
print(x)
```
    1.1

Float value 1.1 is stored in x so data type of variable is *float*. We check it as follows,

```
type(x)
```
    float

3.4.2 Adding any number

Here we assigned the integer value *55* to the variable *length,*

```
length=55
```

You ask python to increase the length by *45,* the python refers to original value of length, which is *55* and add *45* to it.

```
print(length+45)
```
    100

Here is another example, as the integer value *190* assigned to the variable *original_value* and integer value *10* assigned to another variable *new_value*. Both variables added to another variable *result*. The *result* now has a value of *200*.So when we print the variable result then the output will be **200**.

```
original_value=190
new_value=10
```

```
result=original_value+new_value
```

```
print(result)
```
200

Task: Assign the integer value 5000 to the variable *total*. Then, assign another variable and name it *profit*. In profit, subtract integer value 497 from total and print variable *profit.*

Chapter 4

Math Expressions

We will cover all math expression supported by Python in this chapter.

Python language supports the following types of operators.

- Arithmetic Operators
- Comparison (Relational) Operators
- Assignment Operators
- Logical Operators
- Bitwise Operators
- Membership Operators
- Identity Operators

We will look on all operators one by one.

4.1 Arithmetic operator

We will cover this topic in two main parts,

- Familiar operators
- Unfamiliar operators

4.1.1 Familiar Arithmetic operators

We all are familiar with these basic arithmetic operators in maths like addition (+), subtraction (-), multiplication (*) and division (/).

Knowledge:

Suppose we have two variables a and b .We assigned them with values as **a**=10 and **b**=20

- Add operator (+) adds values on either side of the operator (**a+b**=30)
- Subtract operator(-)subtract right hand operand from left hand operand(**a-b**=-10)
- Multiplication operator (*) multiple values on either side of the operator(**a*b**=200)
- Division operator (/) divides left hand operand by right hand operand.(**b/a**=2)

We can use these operators with variables or direct with the data type

i-e integer or float.

In the following, we assigned the value of **36** to variable **var1** and **14** to another variable **var2,**

```
var1=36
var2=14
```

By using '**+**' operator between them it will give us the integer value **50** as follows,

```
print(var1+var2)
```

50

Here we assign values *1* and *2.5* to the variables named **Integer** and **float**. As these are two different data types so it will give us the result in float.

```
Integer=1
float=2.5
result_of_both=Integer+float
```

```
print(result_of_both)
```
3.5

Remember: Whenever there is any float value in the expression the result will be in float.

Multiplication operator also works same as **add** operator. For example,

```
a=2
b=3
mul=a*b
print(mul)
```
6

So last come division in python.

Here we have two variables **var1** and **var2** .Both having integer value **100**

```
val1=100
val2=100
```

Well, you might think that *100* is divided by same number *100* ,so the answer should equals to 1.But when we divide them it will give us the result in data type float as follows,

```
result=val1/val2
print(result)
```

1.0

It is *1.0* which is floating point. It is because python by default do floating point division.

Well, you see how simple is to use these operators.

Task: Do some work by using subtract operator.

4.1.2 Removing ambiguity

Till now, we looked simple arithmetic expressions in which there is one operator at a time. What if there will more operators making the expression more complex? Like,

Result = 2 + 3 * 4 − 5

The order in which we do arithmetic will change the value of the result.

Like, if we first add **2** to **3**, multiply it with **4** and take away **5** from the answer we will get integer value of **15**.

Similarly, if we follow other way by first multiplication of **3** and **4** then adding **2** and at last subtract value of **5** from it. Then the result will be equals to **14**.

As python follows same rule as algebra i-e *precedence rules* but don't worry, we do not have to memorize it. We can eliminate this ambiguity by just using the parentheses. Now we can write it as

Result= 2 + (3 * 4) - 5

First, it will solve the expression inside the parentheses and after that it will solve the remaining expression .It gives us the integer value 9.

Let's look into another example,

Here we have variable **total**, As total equals to **2 + (4 * 5) * 3**.Now it will do multiplication first because of the parentheses but what after that ? Now it adds 2 then multiply by 3 or first multiply it with 3 than adds the integer 2 to it? As, both these cases will give us different result. The solution of these types of problem is to **use more parentheses** like as follows,

```
2+((4*5)*3)
```

62

Now, it first solve inside first parentheses gives **20** then multiply it with **3** gives **60** and then finally add **2** in it.

4.1.3 Unfamiliar Arithmetic operator

Here we have a list of other arithmetic operators that may be new to you.

Operator	Description	Syntax
//	Floor division	a//b

%	Modulus	a%b
**	Exponentiation	a**b

We will see all of them one by one.

4.1.3.1 Floor division

We see above that by dividing one integer to another integer will give us the result in float data type. If we want our answer in integer data type we will use // operator .This division is called integer division. Recall the previous example,

```
val1=100
val2=100
```

```
result=val1//val2
print(result)
```

   1

Information: the // operator discard the decimal part of the value.

For example,

```
x=9
y=10
```

As, 9/10 is equal to 0.9.but Look!

```
x=9
y=10
```

```
result=x//y
print(result)
```

  0

It cuts off the decimal part which is *.9* from the result and gives us only integer part of the result.

So sometimes it might not be useful because information will be lost.

4.1.3.2 Modulus

This operator divides one number by another number, but does not gives you the result of the division. It gives you the remainder after dividing first number by the second number. First, we will declare two variables, *a* and *b*. After that we assigned them with integer values *10* and *5* as in the following,

```
a=10
b=5
result=a%b
print(result)
```

  0

Here by dividing *10* by *5*, the result is *0* because there is no remainder left.

4.1.3.3 Exponentiation

There are two values in this operator. The number to be multiplied by itself is called the ***base*** and the number of times it is to be multiplied is the **exponent**. We assigned them integer value **2** and **3**.It will give us the result by calculating **2** by the power of **3** as follows,

```
base=2
exponent=3
result=base**exponent
print(result)
```

8

4.2 Assignment operators

Here we have table of assignment operation,

Operator	Description	Example
=	Assignment	a=10
+=	Addition shorthand	a+=2(same as a=a+2)
-=	Subtraction shorthand	a-=2(same as a=a-2)
*=	Multiplication shorthand	a*=2(same as a=a*2)
/=	Division shorthand	a/=2(same as a=a/2)
%	Modulus shorthand	a%=2(same as a=a%2)
**=	Exponent shorthand	a**=2(same as a=a**2)
//=	Floor shorthand	a//=2(same as a=a//2)

Looking the following example in which we assign a integer value of **5** to the variable **a** and add the value of **3** to it.

```
a=5
a+=3
print(a)
```

8

The original value of **a,** is **5** which adds **3** to it and prints the result. It works same as below,

```
a=5
a=a+3
print(a)
```

8

Also, we can add some variable instead of using direct integer. Here we declare new variable **value_to_be_add** .We assign it with integer value **3**. Now we add new variable to the original variable **a**. We write it as follows,

```
a=5
value_to_be_add=3
a+=value_to_be_add
print(a)
```

8

Similarly, we can do other operations same as above.

Here we subtract integer value **3** from the original value. Similarly, in the next block we multiply integer **3** with original value **5** which gives us integer value **15**

```
a=5
a-=3
print(a)
```

2

```
a=5
a*=3
print(a)
```

15

Task: Do all the remaining assignment operators

4.3 Bitwise Operators

Here we have different types of Bitwise operators as describes in the following table,

Operator	Description	Example
&=	Bitwise AND shorthand	a&=2(same as a=a&2
|=	Bitwise OR shorthand	a|=2(same as a=a|2)
^=	Bitwise EOR shorthand	a^=2(same as a=a^2)
>>=	Binary Right shift	a>>=2(same as a=a>>2)
<<=	Binary Left shift	a<<=2(same as a=a<<2)

Now, we will see examples of Bitwise operators. In bitwise operator, integer value changes to binary. After that it will perform operation and convert the binary, back to integer.

Let suppose we declare a variable *a* and assigned the value *4* to it.

$$a = 4$$

Now we perform bitwise **AND** operation as follows,

```
a = 4
a &= 2
print(a)
```

```
0
```

As **4** in binary equals to **00000100** and *2* in binary is equals to **00000010**. Now it will perform **and** operations like this.

00000010

00000100

00000000

Also we perform bitwise **OR** operation.

```
a = 5
a |= 3
print(a)
```

7

As, it prints the above result after doing *OR* operation.

A	b	AND(&)	OR(|)	EOR(^)	NOT(~a)
0	0	0	0	0	1
0	1	0	1	1	1
1	0	0	1	1	0
1	1	1	1	0	0

Task: Perform *EOR* and *NOT* operation.

Now we declare a variable *a.* We assigned the value of *60* to *a.* As in binary 60 equals to **00111100**.When we perform left binary shift equal to *2,* then it will become **11110000** which is *240* in decimal.

```
a = 60
print(a << 2)
```

240

Similarly, we can also perform binary right shift as follows,

```
a = 60
print(a >> 2)
```

15

4.4 Comparison operators

We have different types of comparison operators as describes in the following table.

Operator	Description	Example
==	Equal	a==b
!=	Not equal to	a!=b
>	Greater than	a>b
<	Less than	a<b
>=	Greater than or equal to	a>=b

<=	Less than or equal to	a<=b

We will see each of the operators. First have a look on equality operator ==. This operator can be used to compare a variable with a,

- variable
- math expression
- string
- number

> 💡 **Remember:** Equality operator is case sensitive means that "BLACK" is not equals to "black"

Next come, **not equal** operator. The **not equal** operator is opposite to equality operator. Like equality operator it can compare variable with a variable, a variable with any math expression, a variable with a string, a variable with the number or a variable with the combination.

Also this operation is also sensitive so it is true that **BLACK! = black**

In the following example, we have assigned integer value **6** to the variable **dice_roll**. Now **if statement** will check the condition. As it is not equals to **6** satisfies the equation which prints the message "Roll the dice again".

```
dice_roll=3
if dice_roll!=6:
    print("Roll the dice again")
```

Roll the dice again

Here we have the remaining comparison operators, all the following conditions are true

if 10 > 5:

if 5 < 10:

if 10 >= 5:

if 10 >= 10:

if 5 <= 10:

if 10 <= 10:

4.5 Logical operators

We have three logic operators as describes in the following table:

Operator	Description	Example
or	True when either statement is True	a<2 or b>5
and	Only True all given statements are true	a<2 and b>5
not	Reverse the result. If result is true then false and vice versa	Not(a<2)

As *or* operator returns the **True** when one of the statement is true. Here we assigned integer **6** to the variable **x**. It checks the given conditions. As, **6** is greater than **0** but is not smaller than **5** so it returns **True** because one of the condition is True.

```
x=6
print(x>0 or x<5)
```

True

Now see what *and* operator do. As it returns the **True** when, both of the statements are true. Now we assigned different integer to the variable **x**. It also checks the statements. As, *3* is greater than *0* and less than *5* so it returns *True* because both condition are true.

```
x=3
print(x>0 and x<5)
```

True

Not operator will reserve the result and prints **True** when result is false and prints **False** when the result is true. For example,

```
x=4
print(not(x>0 and x<5))
```

False

The above code checks the first condition and satisfied the condition. Similarly, it will check second condition which also satisfied. As **4** is greater than **0** and less than **5.** The result of inner parentheses is **True** but, **not** operator reversed the result and turns it to **False.**

Task: Apply **not operator** with **or operator** and note the result

4.6 Identity Operator

Here we have two types of Identity operators as describes in the following table,

Operator	Description	Example
is	Returns True only when both variable are same objects	a is b
is not	Returns True only when both variable are not same objects	a is not b

First we will discuss **is** operator. Let's suppose we have two list *a* and *b*. Both list stored same items i-e *red* and *green*.

```
a=["red","green"]
b=["red","green"]
```

Now we check *is* operator as follows,

```
print(a is b)
```
```
False
```

It returns **False** because *a* is not the same object as *b,* even both these list having same items.

Now we declare variable *c*. The variable *c* is equal to the list .Now *c* also starts pointing to the list *a*.

```
c=a
```

Now we apply **is** operator,

```
print(a is c)
```
```
True
```

It returns **True** because c is same object as *a*.

Now you might think that **is operator** do same as **==** operator. So what's the difference between them?

Well, to demonstrate the difference between them we simply apply **==** instead of **is** operator. We will get the result **True** as follows,

```
print(a == b)
```

True

It returns **True** because both having same variable store in them.

Now again consider above lists *a* and *b* .We will see that what *is not operator* do,

```
a=["red","green"]
b=["red","green"]
```

```
c=a
```

First we print,

```
print(a is not b)
```

True

It returns **True** because *a* and *b* are not same objects. Although they have same items stored in them i-e *red* and *green*

```
print(a is not c)
```

False

Similarly, it returns **False** because *a* and *c* are not same objects.

At last we see the difference between **!=** operator and **is not** operator. As it returns **False** by applying **!=** operator .

```
print(a != b)
```

False

4.7 Membership Operators

Look at the following table which consists of two types of membership operators,

Operator	Description	Example
in	Returns True if a sequence with the specified values is present in the object	a in b
not in	Returns True if a sequence with the specified values is present in not the object	a not in b

The membership operators will return **True,** if the item present in the list otherwise it returns **False.** Now we have a list of names of students who passed the exam.

```
student_names=["Alif","Ben","Sarah"]
```

Now we have to check whether *John* is in the list. To check we code as follows,

```
print("John" in student_names)
```

```
False
```

As member *Sarah* is in the list. So when we check by using *in* operator then, it returns **True**.

```
print("Sarah" in student_names)
```

```
True
```

We can use other membership operator **not in**. As **not in** will returns **True** only when the item is not in the list. Like, *John* is the student who is not included in the list. So by checking this we will get **True**.

```
print("John" not in student_names)
```

```
True
```

Finally, we checked the item *Sarah*. As it is in the list so **not in** operator will return **False**.

```
print("Sarah" not in student_names)
```

```
False
```

Chapter 5

User Input

Whenever we want to take input from the user/keyboard we use keyword *input()*. Input has an optional parameter, which is prompt string.

5.1 User Input as a variable

When the following block executes, it ask you for the input. For example,

```
Name=input("Enter your name")
```
```
Enter your name
```

Suppose user enters *Jerry*. Now we can print the variable to check what stores inside it.

```
print(Name)
```
```
Jerry
```

It stores the name *Jerry* in the variable *Name.*

Now you can write any name you want. As Jerry is the string you can check it by following command.

```
type(Name)
```
```
str
```

Okay, what if you give a number to the input. For example, here we have a variable **Yours_favorite_number** which is user define. When the block executes the box appears, as follows

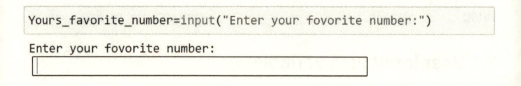

```
Yours_favorite_number=input("Enter your fovorite number:")
```
Enter your fovorite number:
```
|
```

Suppose we entered the integer value **6.** We can check this variable by the following,

```
print(Yours_favoriate_number)
```
6

Great! Let's check the data type of this variable,

```
type(Yours_favorite_number)
```
str

Are you confused ?As you entered integer but it showing the string data type .You can change its data type by type casting

Remember: When we input from user whether it is a number or string always store in string form.

5.2 Type casting

If we really want to store a number in data type **integer,** to compare it with the other integers or we want to perform different operations like we want to add it by other integer.

Here we give integer value of **99** to the variable **data** and check the type

```
type(data)
```

str

5.2.1 String to integer

We can change data type of string into integer by **int()**

```
Str_to_int=int(data)
type(Str_to_int)
```

int

Task: Create a user define variable **number**. Enter integer value 55.

Check the data type which is string. Convert the data type to integer.

5.2.2 Integer to string

Similarly, we can also change back to string data type by using **str()**.

The following output shows the data type of variable **Str_to_int** ,

```
Int_to_str=str(Str_to_int)
type(Int_to_str)
```

str

5.2.3 Integer to float

At last we convert integer to float by using **float()**

```
Int_to_float=float(Str_to_int)
type(Int_to_float)
```

float

Task: Define variable **x**. Assign the integer value 65 to it. Now convert the data type to float.

Chapter 6

Condition Statements

Conditional Statement is one of the most important concepts in Python. It checks that whether the given statements need to be executed or not.

It works by checking the condition for that certain statement, if the condition is true, then the set of code inside the body of statement will be executed.

There are following types of conditional statements in python:

- if
- if-else
- elif
- Nested if / Nested if-else

We will discuss one by one each of its types.

6.1 If statement

In the programming languages, *if statement* is one of the most commonly used conditional statement .If statement is used for decision making. It will run through its body only when the statement is true.

Syntax: First, we use key word *if* then write an expression, which we want to check. End the line with colon (:) as follows

if expression:

Remember: When using reserved word *if*, do not forget to put the colon (:). After colon, the body will starts .You will notice that the cursor is not exactly below to the keyword *if* but have some space left, this is called an indentation. The main purpose of indent is to understand the structure of programme and by this, readability of programme become easy.

Let's do an example. Here we define variables *a, b* and assign integer values *10* and *20*. Then we use *if* statement. We write the condition inside parenthesis and here we check the condition by using an operator i-e < as follows,

```
a=10
b=20
if (a<b):
    print("a is less than b")
```
a is less than b

As the value we assigned to variable *a* is *10* which is less than the value which we assigned to the variable *b* i-e *20*.

So, the condition *a<b* becomes true, result in the execution of the print statement written inside the body.

Remember: The block of if statement is only executes when the given condition is returns true.

Here, the condition of **if** statement is true as before. So it prints the code which is in the body of if statement. When the text is intended, means it is the part of **if** body

```
a=10
b=20
```

we get the following output,

```
if (a<b):
    print("a is less than b")
    print("a is not equal to b")
print("a is not greater than b")
```
```
a is less than b
a is not equal to b
a is not greater than b
```

In the above example, as the condition returns true, it prints all the statements inside the block one by one. But look, last **print** statement is not inside the body so how it prints? Well, after executing all the statement in the body the block will end .After that the interpreter comes to the last line and execute it.

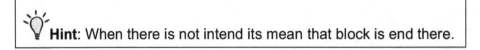
Hint: When there is not intend its mean that block is end there.

Look to the following example. Here the integer value *100* assigned to variable *num1* and integer value *200* assigned to variable *num2*.As the condition of *if* statement returns false so the body will not executed.

```
num1=100
num2=200
if num1>num2:
    print("hello python")
```

Again, what if something is present outside of the body? It will print regardless that the condition is satisfy or not as follows

```
num1=100
num2=200
if num1>num2:
    print("hello python")
print("I am your new user")
```

```
I am your new user
```

The print statement executed which is written outside the body of *if* statement.

6.2 If-else statement

The if-else is usually used when we have to check one statement on the basis of other statement.

It means that if the condition of one statement will not satisfy then there is another statement which will satisfy for the same condition.

For example, if we are defining two variables **number 1, number 2** and assigned two different values to them. We can check the condition *number 1 is greater than number 2* by using operator. If the condition satisfy than print "*number 1 is greater than number 2*" and if this condition is not satisfied then print the following message

"*number 2 is greater than number 1*"

Which, we can write in else block.

Let's do an example related to if-else condition. In the following code, we have variable **Name**, which takes input from user as follows,

```
name=input("Enter your name:")
if (name =="Ainne"):
    print("Welcome!")
else:
    print("Get away from my computer")
```

Enter your name:

We put the condition that if the string value equal to **Ainne,** then execute **if block** which print "Welcome!".

```
Enter your name:Ainne
Welcome!
```

Otherwise, print the statement "Get away from my computer".

```
Enter your name:John
Get away from my computer
```

Recalling the previous example, in which we assigned two different values for both variables **num1** and **num2** and use the if statement to check the condition as follows,

```
num1=input("Enter number 1:")
num2=input("Enter number 2:")
if (num1 < num2):
    print("Number 1 is less than number 2")
else:
    print("Number 2 is less than number 1")
```

Now if we assigned values **4** and **5** to **num1** and **num2** then it prints the statement as follows,

```
Enter number 1:4
Enter number 2:5
Number 1 is less than number 2
```

Great!

Knowledge: To execute conditional statement we can use minimum number of lines to write a code. Instead of executing each line of code python allows us to write in single line.

6.2.1 Minimal line code

For the same example discussed above, we can rewrite the code as follows,

```
a=input("Enter value for a:")
b=input("Enter value for b:")
result="a is less than b" if(a<b) else"a is not less than b"
print(result)
```

Now when this block executed it ask for input value. Let suppose we entered integer value 4 and 3 so we will get the following output.

```
Enter value for a:4
Enter value for b:3
a is not less than b
```

Great! It gives us correct output

But, what happened if we assigned same values for both of the variables?

The **if-else condition** does not work when we have similar input values. For example, if we entered integer value *8* for *num1* and also integer value *8* for *num 2* ,

```
Enter number 1:8
Enter number 2:8
Number 2 is less than number 1
```

Oops! It is not correct answer. We can correct this type of problems in the following method.

6.3 The elif Statement

The python we use short form of else if or elseif as elif. We use **"elif"** statement, when we have to print out the third condition or when the other defined conditions get wrong or incorrect as described in previous topic. Look at the following block of code, in which we add another block i-e *elif,*

```python
num1=input("Enter number 1:")
num2=input("Enter number 2:")
if (num1 < num2):
    print("Number 1 is less than number 2")
elif (num1> num2):
    print("Number 2 is less than number 1")
else:
    print("Both the numbers having equal value")
```

Now if we entered same integer value **8** for both variables **num1** and **num2**

If statement checks for condition **num1 < num2** which is **False** in this case. Then it checks **elif** statement **num1 > num2** which is also incorrect in this case. Then the flow of program control goes to the **else** condition. It checks whether **x==y** which is true so it block will be executed and prints the statement. "Both the numbers are having equal value".

So the output we get, is as follows,

```
Enter number 1:8
Enter number 2:8
Both the numbers having equal value
```

Task: Create a user define variable **total.** If **total** has the value less than or equal to 50 print "Fail". If **total** has the value less than or equal to 70 print "Satisfactory". Otherwise print "Well done"

6.4 Nested if else statement

When we write, if else statement inside the body of another "if" or "else" then this is called **nested if else**.

Let's do an example. Here we have a block of code in which, we defined a variables *country*, and *product_price. Both variables take input from user.*

Then, we created **elif** statement. Inside if block we have nested **elif** statement and inside **elif** block we see another **if else** statement as follows ,

```python
country = input("Enter your country name: ")
products_price=int(input("Enter the cost of the products:"))
if country == "US":
    if products_price <= 50:
        print("Shipping Cost is  $50")
    elif products_price <= 100:
        print("Shipping Cost is $25")
    elif products_price <= 150:
        print("Shipping Costs $5")
    else:
        print("FREE")
elif country == "Uk":
    if products_price <= 100:
        print("Shipping Cost is  $100")
    else:
        print("Free")
else:
        print("Sorry! We deliver our products only in US and Uk")
```

When we run the code, we get the following block. Let's suppose user writes **US ,**

```
Enter your country name:
US
```

When user enters the input, he gets another block as follows,

```
Enter the cost of the products:
100
```

The condition of if statement returns **True**, i-e "US" == "US", which allows the execution of inner block. As user enters the cost of products equal to **100**.The **if** Statement checks for condition **products_price<=50** which is **False** in this case. Then it checks **elif** statement, **products_price<=100** which is true so block will be executed and prints the statement, " Shipping Cost is $25 ".

```
Enter your country name: US
Enter the cost of the products:100
Shipping Cost is $25
```

If another user, type **Canada** for variable **Country** and **458** for **product_price** then, **if** Statement checks for condition **Country = "US"** which is **False** in this case. Then it checks **elif** statement **Country = "Uk"** which is also incorrect in this case. Then, the flow of program control goes to the **else** condition and prints the statement. "Sorry! We deliver our products only in US and Uk"

It gives the output as follows,

```
Enter your country name: Canada
Enter the cost of the products:458
Sorry! We deliver our products only in US and Uk
```

Task: Create two user defined variables *nationality* and *age*. If the variable **nationality** is "UK" and variable **age** is less than or equals 18 print "Sorry. You can't apply". If it's less than or equals to 45 then print "You can work 40 hours a week" otherwise, print "You can only work 18 hours a week"

Chapter 7

Comments

Comment is basically line of codes that python ignores. Comment is only for human not for the machines. We write comment, so other programmer can easily understand the programme. Also comment can figure out your code, when you come back to it a month or a year later.

We write comments between the programme, but it is not readable by the interpreter.

7.1 Types of comments

The following are the types of comment.

7.1.1 Single Line Comment

A single line can be commented by using **#** symbol. In the following code, first we define two variables *m1* and *m2* and assigned them integer values *10* and *2.* We add and subtract both variables and comment both print statements, as follows

```
m1=10
m2=2
print(m1+m2) # adding m1 and m2
print(m1-m2) # subtracting m1 and m2
```

7.1.2 Multiple Line/Paragraph Comment

Multiples line can be commented by using triple quote (""" """).

Recalling the above example, now we comment multiple lines instead of single line comment as follows,

```
m1=10
m2=2
print(m1+m2)
print(m1-m2)
'''Here we define a variable and assign the value to a variable
and do some operations'''
```

Interpreter can't read these comment lines, so doesn't make any error.

Task: Code a 1-line comment. Then write a line of live code that assigns integer value *54* to a variable *number.*

Chapter 8

Lists

Let review the basic concept from chapter **variable**. You see that if we assign integer value of **5** to any variable. And again assign value of **10** to the same variable the previous value is over write.

Just think, if we want to create hundred values and assign them to the different variables then it seems so difficult to remember these variables.

But, what if we assign all values to the same variable?

In python, list is a data structure which is changeable, mutable (i-e can be updated) but ordered sequence of elements.

We can put as much elements as we want. Each element of list is called an **item**.

Syntax:

List having values in square bracket **[ ]** separated by comma **(,)**

list_name=["first_value", "second_value"]

We can store string, Integer or float in the list as following,

```
Names=["Anna","Ben","Brent"]
Grades=[6,7,8]
float_points=[2.39,3.3,4.51,6.7]
```

Also we can store different data types in one list. For example,

```
all=["John",3,3.44]
```

Rules for naming the List is same as naming variable .We can give any name by using letters, numbers, and underscores(to avoid spaces). As first character of name cannot be a number.

8.1 Common List Operations

We can do these operations in the list.

- Access value
- Slicing the elements from list
- Adding new value
- Find the index of a value in list
- Deleting and removing the elements from list
- Popping elements from the list

We will see each operation one by one.

8.1.1 Accessing value from a list

We can access any item by its index number. Each item in the list has its own index number.

Suppose, we have the following list

```
a_list=["Canna",55,3.44,"Dubai",2]
```

Let's try to access first element in the list

```
a_list[1]
```
55

What's wrong? We try to access first element but it gives us second element.

The reason is that indexing by default starts from **0**. It means that element having fifth position in the list must have an index of 4.So for the above example to access first element we pass index 0

 Remember: Index is always 1 less than the member position.

```
a_list[0]
```
55

Checking length of a list

We can check members in a group by function *len()* as follows,

```
len(a_list)
```
5

Great, *len()* function will give us value of **5** as we have five members in the list named *a_list* .

8.1.2 Slicing the elements from list

Let's see a new list of *countries,*

```
countries=["America","Spain","Pakistan","China","Italy"]
```

Now this time we want to access first three elements of the list at the same time. To do this we specify the range of the index.

Syntax: List name then in square we put colon between two indexes.

list_name[starting_index:ending_index]

```
countries[0:3]
```
['America', 'Spain', 'Pakistan']

Now one thing to be noted that if we give range from *0* to *3* then the member *China* is not in the output console because it does not include the last element. If we want to access the member *China* we have to give the end limit of 4.

> **Remember:** First index value represents the start while the last index value represents the position until which we want the value.

Now, if the first index of slicing is first element of the list we can omit the index. For example,

```
countries[:3]
```
['America', 'Spain', 'Pakistan']

It gives same result as **countries [0:3].**

Similarly, if we want to slice till the last element we can surely omit the second index. Here we want to slice the values from index **2** to the end. So we can write as follows,

```
countries[2:]
```

```
['Pakistan', 'China', 'Italy']
```

It gives same result as **countries [2:5]**

8.1.3 Adding

Let's think you make a list having multiple items inside it. If you forgot to add any item in the list or want to add new item in the original list then you can easily add.

8.1.3.1 Adding an item to list

It adds only one element to the existing list.

At the end /tail of list

Once again looking the previous example, where we have list of countries as follows,

```
countries=["America","Spain","Pakistan","China","Italy"]
```

If we want to add new country to the same list countries we use the function of **append().**This function will take the value and add to the last of the original list. For example,

Syntax: First write list name then dot **(.)** and then function *append()*

list_name.append(value_to_be_added)

To add the country **Oman** in the list we write as follows

```
countries.append("Oman")
```

Now, if we want to check element in the list countries we will get following content,

```
print(countries)
```
```
['America', 'Spain', 'Pakistan', 'China', 'Italy', 'Oman']
```

Here new member *Oman* added in the end of the list

Remember: Append function by default add the new element to the last of original list.

Add at the given index of list

Instead of adding element to the last we can append it where we want to. For example, we have a list of even numbers in the following,

```
even_numbers=[0,2,4,8,10]
```

We use *insert()* function to add the element. This function asks what to add? And where to insert the new element ?

```
even_numbers.insert(3,6)
```

The first value of *3* shows the **index position** where we want to insert a value of *6*.Now lets check the list,

```
even_numbers
```

```
[0, 2, 4, 6, 8, 10]
```

Great! It adds the new integer *6* to index *3* of the original list. As, integer *8* now having index value **4.**

8.1.3.2 Adding multiple values to list

We see that the function *append()* and *exert()* add single value to the list but if we want to add multiples values to the list what we can do?

Well, for adding multiple values we use a function of *extend()*.This function add more than one value to the last of original list. For example, in the following we have list of fruits,

```
Fruits=["apple","orange","mango"]
```

We are adding list of fruits to original list fruits as following,

```
Fruits.extend(["stawberry","banana"])
```

The list *Fruits* gives us the following output,

```
print(Fruits)
```

```
['apple', 'orange', 'mango', 'stawberry', 'banana']
```

We can use alternative way of adding the elements in the list as following,

```
Fruits=Fruits+["stawberry","banana"]
```

Here we add a list of new Fruits to the original list without using a function **extend()**.

```
print(Fruits)
```
```
['apple', 'orange', 'mango', 'stawberry', 'banana']
```

Now if we want to see that how many times the item is in the list we use the function **count()**.This function return the occurrences of value in the list for example we have list of random numbers.

```
list=[4,2,6,5,3,6,8,10,20,33,1,8,6]
```

To check many time the value of **6** occur in the list we write as follows,

```
list.count(6)
```
```
3
```

It shows that value of **6** is present 3 times in the list. Also, we can check for the integer **8.**

```
list.count(8)
```

2

Yes it occurs two times in the list. Similarly, if no value is present in the list it will give us **0**.

```
list.count(80)
```

0

8.1.4 Finding the index

We can get index value of any member in the list by using the function *index()*.

This function returns the index value for that item. For example, we have following list of different data types,

```
x=[22,3,4.56,"London",3,"Ben",8.5,1]
```

Now we can check index value of the item **22** by writing the following command,

```
x.index(22)
```

0

It shows that member **22** having index value **0**. Let's check the index value of item **3**

```
x.index(3)
```

```
1
```

As the member **3** occurs two time in the list i-e At index **1** and at index **4**. But function index only return first index value which is **1**.

Similarly, if no value exists in the list then it will give value error that item is not in the list.

💡 **Key:** To check if a particular item exists or not in list we can use if loop as follows:

```
list=[4,2,6,5,3,6,8,10,20,33,1,8,6]
if 5 in list:
    print("Yes")
```

```
Yes
```

Now if we want to clear members from the list we use function **clear()**. This function removes all the members permanent. Here we have a list **all** having 8 members

```
all=["John",5,95,2.55,"Home","Sweet",55,1.3]
```

We run function **clear()** on the list.

```
all.clear()
```

All the member remove and we have now empty list,

```
print(all)
```

```
[]
```

Here you see list name *colors* having three color names,

```
colors=["red","green","blue"]
```

We copy list *colors* to another list named as *colors2*

```
colors2=colors.copy() #by value
```

And *color 2* copies all the members of list colors

```
print(colors2)
```

```
['red', 'green', 'blue']
```

Now, we copy again *colors* to a list named as *colors3*

```
colors3=colors #by reference
```

Look, *color3* having same members as *colors*

```
print(colors3)
```

```
['red', 'green', 'blue']
```

So what's the difference?

As the function *copy()* copy all the members of list by value and other copy members by reference. Let explore more.

As c*olors3* also point out the same list *colors.*

Let's append new item to the list *color*

```
colors.append("yellow")
```

Now check the members in the list *colors3* . You see we append in the list *colors* and new changes also reflect in list *colors3.*

```
print(colors3)
```
```
['red', 'green', 'blue', 'yellow']
```

But not reflect in the list colors2 .As the function *copy()*,don't share the reference,

```
print(colors2)
```
```
['red', 'green', 'blue']
```

We can also join any two list by using **+** operator .Here we have two list *a* and *b*.

```
a=[16,17,18]
b=[20,21,22]
```

We merge both list members into one list *c*

```
c=a+b
```
```
print(c)
```
```
[16, 17, 18, 20, 21, 22]
```

8.1.5 Deleting item of the list

We can remove item from the list by using keyword *del* short for delete

Syntax:

We start syntax with **del,** then space and then write list name with the index of item in square bracket we want to delete.

del list[0]

We can also remove by specifying its value rather than index number.

Syntax:

We start with list name then put a dot then key word **remove ()** and then the value we want to remove enclosed in parenthesis.

list_name.remove(value)

Note one thing, as we deleted item of index zero .Python adjust index number and now integer *17* is on index *0.*

```
print(c)
```
```
[17, 18, 20, 21, 22]
```

8.1.6 Popping elements

We see different methods for removing item from the list. But they remove permanently .We cannot access them anymore .But by using the function *pop()* we can remove the items but we store them to the different list.

Here we have list *com* of different car companies,

```
com=["BMW","Lexus","Toyota","Audi","kia"]
```

We can write as following,

```
popped=com.pop()
print(f"The car which is popped out is {popped}")
print(f"The remaining list is {com}")
```

```
The car which is popped out is kia
The remaining list is ['BMW', 'Lexus', 'Toyota', 'Audi']
```

 Key: Last in, First out. It tell the last element will pop out first

Now the list has four members left. Now, the last element in the list is *Audi*. Now if we run the above cell once again, it popped out last element. Look!

```
popped=com.pop()
print(f"The car which is popped out is {popped}")
print(f"The remaining list is {com}")
```

```
The car which is popped out is Audi
The remaining list is ['BMW', 'Lexus', 'Toyota']
```

Similarly, if one item is left in the list and then again we execute, the list become empty as in the following block,

```
popped=com.pop()
print(f"The car which is popped out is {popped}")
print(f"The remaining list is {com}")
```

```
The car which is popped out is BMW
The remaining list is []
```

What happen now if we want to run the function **pop()** ?As we are left with an empty list. We don't have any item to take out so this will make an error.

💡 **Key:** The function **pop()** by default popped the last values in the list. The function pop() has a feature not only to take out item from the last but also from any index. We can do it by passing the index value.

8.1.7 Sorting the items

Here again we have list of different car companies,

```
com=["BMW","Lexus","Toyota","Audi","kia"]
```

As the elements are randomly placed in the list.

So function **sort()** can be used in the list to sort alphabetically.

```
com.sort()
print(com)
```

```
['Audi', 'BMW', 'Kia', 'Lexus', 'Toyota']
```

💡 **Remember:** The **sort ()** function by default sort the list in the ascending order.

We can also sort in descending order by passing reverse equals to **True** as in the following,

```
com.sort(reverse=True)
print(com)
```

```
['Toyota', 'Lexus', 'Kia', 'BMW', 'Audi']
```

The function *reverse()* reverse the value in the list . Here sorting does not matters. It just reversed the given order. Again, looking to the same list of car companies,

```
com=["BMW","Lexus","Toyota","Audi","kia"]
```

As **BMW** having index value **0, Lexus** having index value **1** and **Kia** having index value of **4.**

```
com.reverse()
print(com)
```

```
['Kia', 'Audi', 'Toyota', 'Lexus', 'BMW']
```

Now **Kia** become first element in the list, **BMW** having index value of **4.**The position of element **Toyota** does not change because it is middle element in the list

Task:

- In the following list, insert a string after "orange

  fruits = ["apple", "orange", "tangerine", "banana"]

- Copy the second through last elements from the list **fruits**
  and assign the slice to the list **x**.

- Sort the list in ascending order.

- Pop the last element from the list x.

- Print the remaining list.

Chapter 9

TUPLE

In python, tuples are like list holdings multiple elements in a single variable except that they are immutable i.e. (data cannot be change or update).

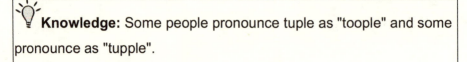

Knowledge: Some people pronounce tuple as "toople" and some pronounce as "tupple".

We cannot add, delete or change values after the creation of tuple instance.

Syntax: First write tuple name, then write values between parenthesis separated by comma,

tuple_name=(value_1,value_2,value_3)

Key:

- Rule for naming of tuple is same as rule for naming a variable or a list.
- The one way of making tuple different from the list is by using the round brackets **()** instead of the square brackets **[ ]**.

9.1 Creating a tuple

Let suppose, we create a list of intelligent students who got good grades in **Wechsler Intelligence Scale for Children** (WISC).Suppose we limit the list to top five students.

Harry, Olivia, Noah ,Leo and Ava

We are so confident that these were the top five students in "2019". Their order won't change and we will never need to replace any of them with any other student. So we make a tuple named **Top_five** as follows,

```
top_five=("Harry","Olivia","Noah","Leo","Ava")
```

Also, if we don't use parentheses it will also store in the form of tuple,

```
top_five="Harry","Olivia","Noah","Leo","Ava"
```

9.1.1 Accessing elements

We can access elements in tuple same as list. Indexing starts from **0** and always end one less than the total elements in the list.

Looking to the above example, we can access the first element by passing index **0,**

```
top_five[0]
```

```
'Harry'
```

And last element by passing index value of **4,**

```
top_five[4]
```

```
'Ava'
```

Also these items have negative index. These negative indexing starts from minus (-) 1 .The **-1** is the index of the last item in the tuple. For example, in the tuple **top_five** we have five members. They all have positive as well as negative index value as follows,

```
#                0         1        2       3      4
   top_five="Harry","Olivia","Noah","Leo","Ava"
#               -5        -4       -3      -2     -1
```

The item at index **0** can also be executed by passing index value minus five as in the following,

```
top_five[-5]
```

```
'Harry'
```

9.1.2 Slicing in tuple

Slicing in tuple works same as works in the list. If we want to see the first three students from a tuple we can write as follows,

```
top_five[0:3]
```

```
('Harry', 'Olivia', 'Noah')
```

Similarly, like list we can also place different data types in the same tuple. For example,

```
atuple=(1,"Hero",33.45,6,"Best")
```

We named tuple *atuple* in which we stored data type *integer, string* and *float*. We write sting values in the quotation marks.

9.1.2 Different operations on tuple

We can concatenate two or more tuples by using **+** operator. For example, we want join two tuples *t1* and *t2* into single tuple t then we write as follows,

```
t1=(1,2,3)   #tuple t1
t2=(4,5,6) #tuple t2
t=t1+t2 # concatenating both t1 and t2
print(t)
```

```
(1, 2, 3, 4, 5, 6)
```

See the value of both tuples move to a single tuple *t.*

We can also find the maximum and minimum values by functions *max()* and *min()* as follows,

```
maxt=max(t)
mint=min(t)
print(f"The maximum value in the tuple is {maxt}")
print(f"The manimum value in the tuple is {mint}")
```

```
The maximum value in the tuple is 6
The manimum value in the tuple is 1
```

As here *6* and *1* are the maximum and minimum values of tuple *t*

We can also iterate a loop in the tuple to print each member in the tuple.

Here we have tuple *x* in which integer values are stored,

```
x=1,2,3
```

We iterate it by using *for loop* as follows,

```
for a in x:
    print(a)
```

```
1
2
3
```

We can check any item existing in tuple as,

```
4 in x
```

False

Because integer value **4** is not in the tuple so it returns **False.**

Now if we want repetition of the result we multiple the tuple name with the number. Here we have string value in a tuple named **x.**

```
x=("Hello ")
```

If we want the output to repeat four times, we simply multiply tuple by 4 using * operator.

```
x*4
```

'Hello Hello Hello Hello '

We can also find the length of a tuple, like the length of a list. We use the function **len()** as follows,

```
len(atuple)
```

5

It shows **atuple** have five elements in it.

We can also see occurrence of any item in a tuple by function **count().** Suppose we have tuple of tossing a coin having random heads and tails represented by **H** and **T.**

```
outcomes=('H','T','T','T','H','H','T','H','H','T','H')
```

Now if we want to count the occurrence of heads in a tuple, then we can write as follows

```
outcomes.count('H')
```

6

Also we can see the occurrence of tails in the list,

```
outcomes.count('T')
```

5

We conclude that head occurs more than the tail.

In list we can **add, modify, remove, delete,** or **pop** but in tuple, we can't do these operations.

As tuples, are **immutable**. If we try to delete last item from the tuple outcomes we get the following error,

```
del outcomes['H']
```

```
-------------------------------------------------------------------
---------
TypeError                                Traceback (most recent c
all last)
<ipython-input-127-f9a7b85b8ae3> in <module>
----> 1 del outcomes['H']

TypeError: 'tuple' object does not support item deletion
```

However to do these operation you have to define the tuple all over again. Or we can do it by the following way.

9.2 Converting tuple into list

First you have to change data type tuple into list by using function *list(),*

```
x=(1,2,3) #tuple x
y=list(x) #Converting into List
print(y)
```

[1, 2, 3]

As we see that it converted into list now we can do operation are applicable which we discussed in the previous chapter **list**.

Now if we want to add a new value **4,** we can do it by using function **append(),**

```
y.append(4)
print(y)
```

[1, 2, 3, 4]
Now we have to convert this list back to the tuple. We will do this by using function **tuple()** as follows,

```
x=tuple(y) #Converting back to tuple
print(x)
```

(1, 2, 3, 4)

Task: Concatenate the second element of tuple **x** with the third element of tuple **y**. In the concatenation include a comma and space in the middle. Assign the concatenated string to a variable.

x=("yellow ", "blue ", " golden ", " silver ", " red ")

y=(" car ", " bike ", " shirt ", " ball ", " sheet ")

Chapter 10

Dictionary in Python

Dictionary means containing a lot of words. As words in a dictionary gives it's meaning or equivalent word (maybe in another language).

Dictionary is a data structure in python. The dictionary may contain zero or multiple elements and those elements are not single value but in pairs which are defined as **key** and **value**. Dictionary can holds multiple values in variable.

Syntax: First we write the name of dictionary (Rule of naming a dictionary is same as rule for naming a variable). In dictionary, we use curly brackets **{ }**. Inside curly bracket, we use pair element which are known as **key** and **value** separated by colon as follows,

dict_name = { Key : value }

If dictionary having multiple pairs then each pair is separated by comma as follows,

dict_name = { Key : value, Key : value Key : value }

10.1 Data type of key and value

The major two elements of a dictionary are **keys** and **values**. We might think that what type of data we can store in these elements of dictionary. Data type of **key** may be **string, integer, float** and whereas the data type of **value** may be **string, integer, float** or a **list** or **tuple** or can be another dictionary.

10.2 Construct a dictionary

Let's start by creating an empty dictionary named **my_dict** as follows,

```
my_dict={}
```

Now make this dictionary useful by defining the keys and their values.

Here we define the string **Name** as a **key** then we use colon. The **value** of the dictionary is also of data type string **John** as follows,

```
my_dict={"Name":"John"}
```

We can define more than one pairs in dictionary as in the following block of code,

```
my_dict={"Name":"John","Age":30}
```

Here the data type of the **value 30** is integer.

> 💡 **Hint**: If we want to execute the value, then we will search for key.

Have a look on another given example. Here first we define an empty dictionary i-e **squares.** Then we define for loop in which it returns the value by multiplying the number itself i-e **x*x**. We get the following output,

```
squares = {}
for x in range(6):
    squares[x] = x*x
print(squares)
```

{0: 0, 1: 1, 2: 4, 3: 9, 4: 16, 5: 25}

Task: Define a dictionary with two items. The keys are "Population" and "Year". The values are numbers. Then print the dictionary.

10.3 Accessing information from Dictionary

We created dictionary in the previous topic. Now if we want to print all keys and values of the dictionary then we can write as follows,

```
print(my_dict)
```

{'Name': 'John', 'Age': 30}

We can access the value by providing the key to the dictionary name. To do this we use the square bracket [ ].If we want to get *John* as the output then, we pass the key i-e *Name* as in the following line,

```
print(my_dict['Name'])
```

John

Or if we want to access the value of Age we can write as follows,

```
print(my_dict['Age'])
```

30

Task: Create a dictionary and name it as "weather". In the dictionary *weather* ,the **keys** are the names of days and **values** are Sunny for keys "Mon" and "Wed", Cloudy for keys "Tues" ,"Thur" and "Fri" and Rainy for keys "Sat" and "Sun". Target the fourth element, and assign its value to the variable Target. At last, print the variable.

 Warning:

If are trying to access any key which is not present in dictionary will raise an expectation of type **Key Error.**

Keys are case sensitive, hence the following statement will throw an expectation of error type. Recalling the previous example, we have a dictionary **my_dict** having keys **Name** and **Age**.

In the following block, we pass the non existing key **Gender** which creates an error

```
print(my_dict['Gender'])
```

```
------------------------------------------------------------
----------
KeyError                              Traceback (most recent c
all last)
<ipython-input-9-ccac26aa4154> in <module>
----> 1 print(my_dict['Gender'])

KeyError: 'Gender'
```

10.4 Length of dictionary

The pairs in the dictionary, tells about the length of the dictionary. We can find length of dictionary easily by using built-in **len()**. In the following, we find the length of dictionary **my_dict**

```
len(my_dict)
```
2

As it consists of two pairs so length equals to 2.

10.5 Adding a new key to existing dictionary

We can easily add a new key to the existing dictionary. When we are assigning a value to the key which does not exists, Python creates the key and assigns the value to the key and if key is already present the value is overwritten. To add key we must follow the following syntax

Syntax: First we write the name of a dictionary in which we want to add. In square brackets **[ ]** we write the name of the key then, write equals sign followed by the value.

dictionary_name [key] = value

Here we have a dictionary named **child. Name, Grade** and **Section** are the **keys** of the dictionary and **John, fifth** and **Purple** are the **values** of the dictionary as below ,

```
child={'Name':'John','Grade':'fifth','Section':'Purple'}
```

Notice that there is no key name as **Father Name**. But we want to add this key to increase the information.

We can write as follows,

```
child ['FatherName']='Alice'
```

Now the key *FatherName* added to the dictionary *child.* We can verify it as follows,

```
print(child)
```
```
{'Name': 'John', 'Grade': 'fifth', 'Section': 'Purple', 'FatherNam
e': 'Alice'}
```

Amazing, we did it.

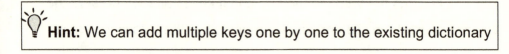
Hint: We can add multiple keys one by one to the existing dictionary

10.6 Updating a key value

Similarly, we can also Up-date any value of key. To update the value we follow the same syntax discussed in the previous topic

dictionary_name [key] = value

Now if we do this for the existing keys then the values of keys are updated. For example, **John** passed the exams and promoted to next grade. So we can easily update the value of key *Grade* as follows,

```
child ['Grade']='Sixth'
```

Let's verify it by printing the dictionary child as follows,

```
print(child)
```

```
{'Name': 'John', 'Grade': 'Sixth', 'Section': 'Purple'}
```

Note that the value for the key *Grade* has change.

> 💡 **Hint:** Same key cannot be two times in a dictionary .Previous key overwrite and latest value is updated in the dictionary.

10.7 Removing information from Dictionary

We created dictionaries, we also learn how to add elements in the existing dictionary. What if we want to remove some element from the dictionary permanently ?

We can easily remove any key by using keyword **del**. We pass the dictionary name along with the key. It can delete the key with its value.

Syntax:

del(dictionary_name [key])

Recalling the previous example again, in which we created a dictionary child having key *Name, Grade* and *Section*. Now we want to remove the key *Grade* from the dictionary child so write as follows,

```
del(child['Grade'])
```

Now when we print child it gives us the following output,

```
print(child)
```
```
{'Name': 'John', 'Section': 'Purple'}
```

Note that the key *Grade* with its value *Sixth* removed from the dictionary.

10.8 Checking the key in the dictionary

To check the specific key in the dictionary we can pass the key, the output will be **True** or **False**.

True tells us that the key exists in the dictionary and False tells us that key is not a part of that dictionary.

Syntax:

Key in dictionary_name

Again in the dictionary child if we want to check for the key *Name*, we write the following,

```
'Name' in child
```
```
True
```

As we deleted the key Grade in previous topic, if we check for *Grade* it must returns **False** as follows,

```
'Grade' in child
```
```
False
```

We can also check the key by using for loop. First we created for loop. Inside for loop we define **if-else statement**. If the given key found then it print the statement "Key found" and the loop breaks.

We check the key Name in the dictionary

```
for item in child:
    if "Name" in child:
        print ("Key found")
        break
    else:
        print ("No keys found")
```
Key found

As the key Name exists so, it returns **Key found.**

10.9 Iterating over information Dictionary

Iteration is the repetition of a process in order to generate a sequence of outcomes.

It means to excess every element in the dictionary. Python provides three methods over dictionary which are

- Values
- Keys
- Key value pairs

We need for loop or while loop for iteration. We will see all the methods one by one.

10.9.1 Accessing Keys of the dictionary

- For accessing all keys present in the dictionary we can use the concept of loop. Here we use for loop. We use the function **.key**

```
for key in child.keys():
    print (key)
```

```
Name
Section
FatherName
```

Task: Create a dictionary consists of at least five items. The keys of dictionary are the names of students and values of dictionary are the percentage of student marks. Create a loop through a dictionary's keys. If a key's value is greater than or equal to 70, display "Yes. You can apply for admission" and break the loop.

10.9.2 Accessing Values of the dictionary

- For accessing all values in the dictionary we again use for loop. The we use the function of **.values** as follows,

```
for value in child.values():
    print (value)
```

```
John
Green
Alice
```

It shows all the values of the keys.

10.9.3 Accessing pairs of the dictionary

- Now if we want complete elements of the dictionary i-e key with the values then we use **for loop**. For accessing all elements we use important function **.items.** In the following, we access pairs of child class.

```
for item in child.items():
    print (item)
```
```
('Name', 'John')
('Section', 'Green')
('FatherName', 'Alice')
```

Great! It shows all the pairs in different tuples.

> **Hint:** Item = { key : value }

Task: Create a dictionary and named it as trip. The keys are Canada, United State, Pakistan, United Kingdom and Armenia, Set the values as any city of these countries. Create for Loop through the keys in a dictionary to test if any of the keys is equal to "United Kingdom". If so, delete that item and break the loop.

(**Hint:** You loop through keys in a dictionary in the same way as you loop through values, by substituting keys.)

10.10 Sorting the dictionary

We have the following dictionary *information* having different values of keys and values. The keys contain names of persons and values of dictionary contain ages of persons.

```
information= {'John':'59','Jerry':'21','Norah':'27','Alex':'51','Phoebe':'52'}
```

Now we can sort out the dictionary keys alphabetically by using method *sort()*.

```
for key, value in sorted(information.items()):
    print (key, value)
```

```
Alex 51
Jerry 21
John 59
Norah 27
Phoebe 52
```

10.11 What you can store in Dictionary

Any data structure can store as value in dictionary. For example

Dictionary can contain,

- List
- Tuple
- Any type primitive or user defined
- Another dictionary as its value
- Or combination of these

10.11.1 List in Dictionary

Till now, we have seen that the dictionary consists of keys and value, Also, learn that how to create these keys and values, how we can add more to the existing dictionary and how we can access them.

Dictionary may contain list of variable. We have a lot of ways to create a dictionary consists of lists. In this topic we will discuss different methods

10.11.1.1 Using Subscript

In this method, first we create an empty dictionary **Children** as the following,

```
children={}
```

Now we want to store the information of more than one child, which we do by using lists. We can add lists as **values** to the above dictionary as follows,

```
children['Name']=['Sarah','Alex']
```

Here the **Name** will be Key of dictionary and **['Sarah' , 'Alex']** will be the values of the dictionary.

Note that, we start with the name similar to the name of empty dictionary i-e **children**

 Hint: We add list using the following syntax,

dictionary_name[key]=[value_1 , value_2]

Similarly, we add another Key *Age* to the same dictionary children as follows,

```
children['Age']=[12, 14]
```

Now, if we print the dictionary children it gives us the following output,

```
print(children)
 {'Name': ['Sarah', 'Alex'], 'Ages': [12, 14]}
```

Great!

Or we can define a dictionary of list as follows,

```
children={'Name':['Sarah','Alex'],'Ages':[12,14]}
```

When we print this, it gives us the following output,

```
print(children)
 {'Name': ['Sarah', 'Alex'], 'Ages': [12, 14]}
```

Note that the output is same.

Knowledge: We can't add the list as the key value in the dictionary.

For example, if we write the values of Name as the key and value of Key as the value then it will gives us the following error

```
children{['Sarah', 'Alex']:[12, 14]}

    File "<ipython-input-16-40c83ac3155a>", line 1
    children{['Sarah', 'Alex']:[12, 14]}
            ^
SyntaxError: invalid syntax
```

10.11.1.2 Adding list as value using append() method

Again, we create empty dictionary **children,**

```
children={}
```

In the following, we added list as the value of the dictionary,

```
children["Names"] = ['Sarah','Alex']
```

Now, we create new list **Names_of children** as follows,

```
children["Names"].append(Names_of_children)
```

We can add this as the nested value of the dictionary using **append()** method as follows,

```
children["Names"].append(Names_of_children)
```

If we print the dictionary children then, it will give us the following output,

```
print(children)
```

```
{'Names': ['Sarah', 'Alex', ['Alan', 'Kate']]}
```

10.11.1.3 Using set default() method

In this method we iterate the list. In every iteration, we keep appending the elements till given range.

We can do this by using *setdefault()* method.

First we created an empty dictionary. Then we created a list having elements i-e *1, 2* and *3.* We iterate the elements in the list by using **for loop** as follows,

```
dictionary = dict()

List = ['1', '2', '3']
for value in List:
    for element in range(int(value), int(value) + 3):
        dictionary.setdefault(element, []).append(value)
```

When we print the dictionary, it will give us the following output,

```
print(dictionary)
```

```
{1: ['1'], 2: ['1', '2'], 3: ['1', '2', '3'], 4: ['2', '3'], 5:
['3']}
```

Note in each iteration, the new value of the list is appending.

10.11.1.4 Using list comprehension

Here we create a dictionary of list, using list compression. We named it as *range* as follows,

```
range = dict((val, range(int(val), int(val) + 2))
                for val in ['1', '2', '3','4'])
```

If we print the dictionary *range* then, we get the output as follows,

```
print(d)
```
```
{'1': range(1, 3), '2': range(2, 4), '3': range(3, 5), '4': range(4, 6)}
```

10.11.1.5 Using defaultdict

First we import the **defaultdict** from collection as follows,

```
from collections import defaultdict
```

We created the list item containing three tuples i-e

(' First ' , 1), (' Second ' , 1) and *(' Third ' , 3)*

```
item = [('First', 1), ('Second', 2), ('Third', 3)]
Dictionary = defaultdict(list)

for key, val in item:
    Dictionary[key].append(val)
```

> **Hint:** We can do the same thing in simple dictionary but, more efficient way is to use *defaultdict.*

We get the following output of the dictionary,

```
print(Dictionary)
```

defaultdict(<class 'list'>, {'First': [1], 'Second': [2], 'Third': [3]})

Now look at the following block, the list item contains three tuples. The first and third tuple containing the same string value for the first element

i-e *First* as in the following block,

```
item = [('First', 1), ('Second', 2), ('First', 3)]
Dictionary = defaultdict(list)

for key, val in item:
    Dictionary[key].append(val)

print(Dictionary)
```

defaultdict(<class 'list'>, {'First': [1, 3], 'Second': [2]})

Hint: The two keys of the dictionary can never be same.

10.11.1.6 Using Json

First we import **json**. Then we create a list containing three tuples. Also we created empty dictionary. We use method *dumps()* as follows,

```
import json
list= [('First', 1), ('Second', 2), ('Third', 3)]
dict={}
hash = json.dumps(list)
dict[hash] = "value"
```

We will get the output as follows,

```
print(dict)
```

```
{'[["First", 1], ["Second", 2], ["Third", 3]]': 'value'}
```

In chapter 19, we will discuss JSON in detail.

Task: In the following you have a dictionary containing list. Test whether "red" is in the list within the dictionary.

Sample = { "colors" : ["green" ,"blue" ,"purple"] }

10.11.1.7 Accessing Values from the Dictionary of list

We created dictionaries having list in it. In this topic, we will learn that how we can extract information from list inside dictionary easily.

Syntax: We access by giving the name of the dictionary then key and then corresponding index. We use Index to access in the list

dictionary_name [key] [index]

Here we have dictionary children containing lists in it,

```
children={'Name':['Sarah','Alex'],'Ages':[12,14]}
```

To get the age at index 1 we can write as follows,

```
print(children['Ages'][1])
```

14

As we see that to access the value of a dictionary we provide key **Age** inside square bracket, in this case the value is a list, so an extra pair of square brackets is used to access the list element.

Similarly, we can also access Name by using following command

```
print(children['Name'][0])
```

```
Sarah
```

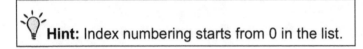
Hint: Index numbering starts from 0 in the list.

10.11.2 Dictionary in a List

We created list in a dictionary. In this topic we will see that how we can create dictionary in a list.

Knowledge: When we create list of dictionary then list will be in memory database and each dictionary object will represent a unique record.

All the members of list will be dictionaries. Let's do an example,

First we created an empty list and named it as **list_of_dictionary**,

```
list_of_dictionary=[]
```

Here we have three dictionaries i-e **dictionary_1, dictionary_2** and **dictionary_3**. Each dictionary has three keys i-e **Name, Gender** and **Age** as following,

```
dictionary_1={'Name':'Alex','Gender':'M','Age':45}
```

Similarly,

```
dictionary_2={'Name':'Lobby','Gender':'F','Age':38}
```

```
dictionary_3={'Name':'Marinda','Gender':'F','Age':61}
```

Now we have to add these three dictionaries in the list by using **append** method as follows,

```
list_of_dictionary.append(dictionary_1)
```

Also, we append second dictionary **dictionary_2** to list as

```
list_of_dictionary.append(dictionary_2)
```

Similarly, appending **dictionary_3**

```
list_of_dictionary.append(dictionary_3)
```

Now we can verify it by checking the list as follows,

```
list_of_dictionary
[{'Name': 'Alex', 'Gender': 'M', 'Age': 45},
 {'Name': 'Lobby', 'Gender': 'F', 'Age': 38},
 {'Name': 'Marinda', 'Gender': 'F', 'Age': 61}]
```

Awesome! **list_of_dictionaries** having three dictionaries as the members of it.

We can also access the dictionaries in list by using **for loop**. We can apply **for loop** as follows,

```
for dictionary in list_of_dictionary:
    print(dictionary)
```

```
{'Name': 'Alex', 'Gender': 'M', 'Age': 45}
{'Name': 'Lobby', 'Gender': 'F', 'Age': 38}
{'Name': 'Marinda', 'Gender': 'F', 'Age': 61}
```

 Hint: Square brackets **[ ]** are used for list and curly **{ }** for dictionaries

10.11.2.1 Accessing information from dictionary in list

We created list of dictionaries. Now we can retrieve the information from it easily.

Hint:

- In list, we access any member through index.
- In dictionary, we access any member through key.

Recalling the previous example, in which we created a list *list_of_dictionary*. This list contains three dictionaries as its member.

Syntax: We access by giving the name of the list then index and then corresponding key .We use Index to access in the list.

list_name [index] [key]

Now if we want to access the *Gender* of second member of the list we can write as follows,

```
print(list_of_dictionary[1]['Gender'])
```

F

Similarly, we can get the value of key *Age* of third member by the following command,

```
print(list_of_dictionary[2]['Age'])
```

61

Great!

Task: Create three dictionaries **model_1 model_2** and **model_3.**

The key **Model** of dictionaries having values i-e **iphone 4, iphone 4S** and **iphone 5** and the values of Key **Year** of these dictionaries are **2010, 2011** and **2012.**

Append these dictionaries to an empty list models. Get the value of third Model and assigned to a variable.

10.11.3 Dictionary in a dictionary

In this section, we will create a dictionary which holds another dictionary or dictionaries.

💡 **Knowledge**: One single dictionary containing collection of dictionaries into it is also known as **nested dictionary**

Syntax: We follow the following syntax,

dictionary_name = {key:{Values}}

Let's do an example of nested dictionary. Here we have a dictionary **Person**, having keys i-e **Name** and **friends**. The key **friends** having values in the form of dictionary

```
Person={'Name':'Elina','friends':{'Annie':{'Age':'10','Class':'6th standard'},
                                   'Alex':{'Age':'8','Class':'4th Standard'}}}
```

Hint: For better understanding of above example,

dictionary_name = { key :value , key : { {value_1} ,{value_2} } }

Remember to add a comma after each curly bracket that closes a dictionary (**}**).

10.11.3.1 Accessing values of dictionary in dictionary

We can easily access the value for the element in the nested dictionary.

Syntax: To access the value of a dictionary we provide key name inside square bracket, in this case the value is a dictionary so, we use extra pair of square brackets to access the further key.

dictionary_name [key][key][key]

Now, we want to get the information about the age of **Annie** which is the value of key **friends** then we write as the follows ,

```
print(Person['friends']['Annie']['Age'])
```

10

 Hint: Focus on the level of target value.

Similarly, if we want to access the Class of Alex then, we write the following line

```
print(Person['friends']['Alex']['Class'])
```

4th Standard

Task: Code a list containing two dictionaries. Each dictionary has two key-value pairs. All keys and values are numbers. Get any value out of dictionary and assign it to a variable. Also print that variable.

Chapter 11

Loop

In general, statements are executed sequentially, first statement executed then second and so on. Now if we want to perform a task multiple times we write it multiple times. There may be a situation when you need to execute a block of code several number of times. For example, if you want to execute your name for fifty times then you have to write the statement **print(name)** fifty times which will definitely take a lot of your time and lines for code.

```
print("John")
print("John")
print("John")
print("John")
    :        :
```

As your task will be completed by using this method but it is not the efficient way of doing this.

Now, let's suppose we have a list of different number and we have to check whether the input value is present in the list or not. In the following we define a variable **Number_to_check** and assign the integer value **7**. Also we have a list **Number_list** having 5 elements in it,

```
Number_to_check = 7
Number_list= [2,6,55,9,7]
```

As there are 5 elements in the list so we have to check it for each element one by one as follows,

```
if Number_to_check == Number_list[0]:
    print("Yes it is in the list")
elif Number_to_check == Number_list[1]:
    print("Yes it is in the list")
elif Number_to_check == Number_list[2]:
    print("Yes it is in the list")
elif Number_to_check == Number_list[3]:
    print("Yes it is in the list")
elif Number_to_check == Number_list[4]:
    print("Yes it is in the list")
```

As the input 7 is already in the list named **Number_list**. So this will give us the output "Yes it is in the list"

💡 **Key**: The efficient way of doing task is by reducing the lines of code and time

---

We have two types of loop i-e **for loop** and **while loop**.

11.1 For Loop

For loop in python is a concise approach. It reduces load of code. The loop iterate over a given sequence which can be a *set, list, tuple* or *dictionary.*

Syntax: We use keyword **for(),** then create a variable then sequence(i-e list) and put colon **(:)** to make a body of loop or intended block.

for a in list:

print(list) # body of for loop

Here, the variable **a** will takes value of item inside the sequence, in every iteration.

We can do previous example using **for loop** and the function **range().** As we have to execute the name for fifty times So, we can write as follows,

```
for a in range(50):
    print("John")
```

It will print the sting *John* fifty times.

> 💡 **Key:** Like indexing, the function **range()** will also create values from **0**. The name will executed fifty times.(i-e 0 to 49). As, *50* will not be included in this range.

As range give values from **0** we can also generate numbers. If we want to prints till 10th number, we do as follows,

```
for a in range(11):
    print(a)
```
```
0
1
2
3
4
5
6
7
8
9
10
```

We give range of 11 so the loop will iterate eleven times starting creating values from **0**. In first iteration the range will create **0** which will initialize to the variable *a*. The **print statement** prints 0.Then in second iteration, function *range()* create **1** assign to variable *a* and prints the value. Similarly, it will prints the values until the iteration get completed. Now if we want to print only values from 1 to 5 we can give the starting and ending point in the range function. We can write as follows,

```
for a in range(1,6):
    print(a)
```

1
2
3
4
5

The loop will execute five times so it prints the values from *1* to *5*.

We can also give optional third parameter to the function **range()** known as step. By default its value is **1**. In the following, we give the value to third parameter equals to **2**. It means that the difference between the two consecutive numbers in the output will equals to 2. Look!

```
for a in range(1,10,2):
    print(a)
```

1
3
5
7
9

First it prints the value *1*, then takes 2 steps and prints the value *3*. Again, it takes two steps and prints *5* and so on.

Similarly, we can also print the counting in the reverse order starting the value of range from 10 to 1 and giving step function with negative value as follows,

```
for a in range(10,1,-2):
    print(a)
```

```
10
8
6
4
2
```

We can perform above task related to **checking the number** in the list by **for loop**. In the following, we have a variable ***Number_to_check*** and list ***Number_list,***

```
Number_to_check = 7
Number_list= [2,6,55,9,7]
```

We apply ***for loop*** as follows,

```
for x in Number_list:
    if Number_to_check == x:
        print("Yes it is in the list")
```

```
Yes it is in the list
```

Important:

- We have three variables in above code. A new variable ***x***, list of number ***Number_list*** and the value we want to check in the list in variable ***Number_to_check.***

- Also, the second line of code is intended because we use colon in first line due to **for loop**. Similarly, third line is also more intended because we use another colon in second line due to **if statement.**

This code pulls up each element in the list **Number_list**,one by one. Note that, we created a variable **x** in which current elements in the list will assigned with each iteration. It then checks this value against the value of the variable **Number_to_check**.

Here we want to check the number **7** which we assigned to the variable name **Number_to_check.**

The **for loop** starts with the first element in the list **Number_list**. It asks, Is this first element **2** in the **Number_list**, equal to the number we are checking for? If No, then the loops moves to second number,**6.** Again it is not equals to **7**. Then loop moves to third, fourth and so on until we found the number equals to **7**. Here fifth number having index_value **4** satisfy the equation. So it displays the message "Yes it is in the list."

11.1.1 Break

If we want loop to find any specific value in the list having large number of items but we also want to terminate our loop when it finds the target value in the list because, after that there is no purpose of continuing the loop. To terminate the loop python provides the keyword **break()**.

For example, we have another list named **int** having different integer values in it as follows,

```
int=[8,2,6,7,5,1,3,9,4]
```

Again, we are looking for number **7** assign to the variable **Number_to_check**. We can write it as follows,

```
for a in int:
    if Number_to_check == a:
        print("Yes it is in the list")
        break
```

```
Yes it is in the list
```

Here the number **7** have index value of **3**.So by using *break*, the loop will be terminated as it encounters 7.

> **Remember:** Loop never stops until and unless we provide any external condition.

Here is another example of keyword **break()**. We want to print the number, which are not divisible by two. So we put a condition that if it's remainder equals to zero than break the loop,

```
for number in [7,9,13,60,77]:
    if (number%2==0):
        break
    print(number)
```

```
7
9
13
```

Here we have list having different integer values. When it comes to the integer value *60* (which is divisible by 2) then, it will break **for loop** and don't print any further value whether it satisfy the condition or not.

11.1.2 Continue

If we want to stops only the current iteration but don't want our loop to be terminated or exit, we use keyword *continue()*.

In the following, we have a list **colors,**

```
colors = ["blue", "black", "red"]
```

Suppose, we don't want color *black* to print. So we use *continue()* to block the iteration for index value 1.

```
for x in colors:
  if x == "black":
      continue
  print(x)
```

blue
red

As the loop don't exists but print all values except item *black* .

Now we see the same example as we discussed in previous topic **break()**. Now we use keyword *continue()* instead of *break().* Iteration in which the condition is satisfy will be skipped as follows,

```
for number in [7,9,13,60,77]:
    if (number%2==0):
        continue
    print(number)
```

7
9
13
77

Here, for loop not printed the value *60* but after that the loop will continue.

Remember: Keyword **break()** breaks the loop permanently whereas keyword continue() skip the loop at certain time.

Looking to another example. Now we assign the city names to a list named *cities* as follows,

```
cities=["New York","Los Angeles","California","Chicago"]
```

We know that we can print each element of the list by using **for loop**.

```
for city in cities:
    print(city)
```

```
New York
Los Angeles
California
Chicago
```

11.1.3 For loop on a variable

Now if we implement the loop on a variable having string value then it prints the character of the string. In the following, we assign string *Chicago* to the variable *city*,

```
city="Chicago"
```

We apply the *for loop* as follows,

```
for a in city:
    print(a)
```

```
C
h
i
c
a
g
o
```

As there is only one value so for loop will assigns first character *C* to the variable *a* and print it. Then assigns second character *h* of string to the variable *a* and print it also and so on.

11.1.4 For loop on a tuple

We can also apply *for loop* on a tuple. We have a tuple name *city* having two values in it as follows,

```
city="Chicago","New York"
```

Now we implement for loop to print the values of the tuple,

```
for a in city:
    print(a)
```

```
Chicago
New York
```

Note that, we get elements of the tuple not characters of elements.

> **Key:** If the list city having two strings then it form a tuple. As in tuple, we can ignore the parenthesis.

Task: Loop through the tuple named vehical having following elements.

car, bike, cycle

If one of the elements has the same value as bike, display "yes"

11.1.5 For loop on User defined input

In this topic, we see that how can we programme to display a multiplication table by using the input from user. We stored the input value in a variable *table_number*. Now by running this block of code we get,

```
table_number=int(input("Enter table number:"))
for s in range(1,11):
    print(f"{table_number}*{s} = {table_number*s}")
```

```
Enter table number:
```

┌───┐
│ | │
└───┘

Hint: We know that the input from user is always in string
datatype() so we convert to integer by typecasting i-e using **int()**

Now, input take value from user and convert it into data type integer.
Then it evaluates the expression inside for loop for ten times as range is
from 1 to 10.

We enter the number **4**.Now **4** is assigned to the variable
table_number. Then **4** is multiplied with the values creating by function
range() which are from **1** to **10**.In this way we get the following
multiplication table,

```
Enter table number:4
4*1 = 4
4*2 = 8
4*3 = 12
4*4 = 16
4*5 = 20
4*6 = 24
4*7 = 28
4*8 = 32
4*9 = 36
4*10 = 40
```

11.1.6 Nested for loop:

The loop within the loop is called **nested loop**. It means that inner loop is in the body of outer loop. There is no restriction of defining the inner loops i-e the nesting level can be defined at n times.

The iteration starts from the outer loop which activates the inner loop. The inner loop executes to completion. After completion, again second iteration of the outer **loop** triggers the inner **loop**. This process repeats until the range of outer **loop** finishes. For example, we have the following block,

```
for a in range(3):
    print("Inner loop begins")
    for char in "Ben":
        print(a,char)
```

When we execute the above block, then the function range will create number *0* which store in the variable *a* .Then it prints the *print()* statement "Inner loop begins" .After that the pointer will move to the second *for()* loop which is in the body of first *for()* loop so whatever is the part of second loop will also execute .

As there is string value in second *for()* loop which means it prints the character of the string one by one. It comes back to the first loop when whole inner body executed. In second iteration, the function *range()* will create value of *1* and assign to the variable *a.* Then prints the *print()* statement .Again it start the execution of second loop. It prints the variable *a* and character of string. The process repeats again. The output is,

```
Inner loop begins
0 B
0 e
0 n
Inner loop begins
1 B
1 e
1 n
Inner loop begins
2 B
2 e
2 n
```

Task:

1) Write a programme to display multiple tables (i-e from 2 to 5) at the same time by using **nested for() loop**

Hint: Range of the outer for() will be 2 and input_value+1 i-e range(2,input_value)

2) Run an inner loop inside an outer loop. If the inner list contains an element with the value of 1, display "ok".

Hint: Remember to indent correctly.

11.2 While loop

This is another type of loop. The while loop works same as *for loop*. The only difference between them is that the while loop allow user to terminate the loop by setting the value of a flag. Flag is just the variable

Here we have example,

```
a=0
while a<=0:
    print("This is while loop printing")
```

```
This is while loop printing
This is while loop printing
This is while loop printing
This is while loop printing
Thi- i- .hil. l--- ---i--i--
```

First we declare a variable *a* and set integer value of *0* to it.

We set the condition of a while loop that if the value of *a* is less than or equals to zero than print the following message

"This is while loop printing"

As value of *a* satisfied the condition so it prints the message infinite time

Here we have similar example which we covered in the topic **for loop.**
This will print the number from **0** to **5**.We can write the while loop as follows:

```
a=0
while a<=5:
    print(a,"This is while loop printing")
    a+=1
```

Again, we declare a variable *a* and assign integer value *0* to it.

Now when loop begins it will prints the print statement as well as it increment the value of variable *a* by *1*. After that, the second iteration started in which the value of variable *a* is updated to *2*. Again it will check the condition. As *2* is also less than *5,* which satisfied the condition and print the statement. After printing it, values updated to *3* and so on.

Now, when value of *a* becomes *6*, the while loop will check the condition. As condition is not satisfied so loop will terminate.

Now the above code gives the output as follows,

```
0 This is while loop printing
1 This is while loop printing
2 This is while loop printing
3 This is while loop printing
4 This is while loop printing
5 This is while loop printing
```

Hint: Output gives us message with the numbering because we write *a* in the print statement. As value of *a* is increasing by *1* in each round.

Task: Set the condition, as long as **x** doesn't equal 99, display **x**, then increment it by 1 using the concise way to increment.

11.2.1 The Break Statement

In break statement, the loop will stop even if the condition of while loop is True

In the following block, we have an example of break statement in while loop

```
i = 1
while i < 6:
    print(i)
    if i == 3:
        break
    i += 1
```

When we execute the code, it gives us the following output,

1
2
3

It exits the loop, when *i* equals to integer value *3.*

Task: Code a **while** loop that loops through the following list.

basic=["wood" , "cement" , "brick", "window"]

When an element in the list is **False**, break the loop.

11.2.2 The Continue Statement

In while loop, the continue statement can stop the specific iteration, and again continue with next iterations.

Recalling the previous example, here we use keyword continue() instead of *break()*

```python
i = 0
while i < 6:
    i += 1
    if i == 3:
        continue
    print(i)
```

Now it gives us the following output,

1
2
4
5
6

11.2.3 The Else Statement

Let's have a look to the given example. Now if we want a loop to print the names of our favourite food. As the favourite foods vary from person to person so it should be user defined input.

```
a=0
while a<=10:
    input("Your favourite food: ")
    a+=1
```

```
Your favourite food:
┌─────────────────────────────────────────────────────┐
│|                                                      │
└─────────────────────────────────────────────────────┘
```

By running the above we will get user defined input box in which user can write the names of his favourite food.

For example, user writes his first favourite food as **Spaghetti Bolognese**. Again it starts the execution of loop for the second time. Then user enters his second favourite food i-e **Thai green curry**

```
Your favourite food: Spaghetti Bolognese

Your favourite food:
┌────────────────────────────────────────────┬──────┐
│ Thai green curry|                           │   ×  │
└────────────────────────────────────────────┴──────┘
```

As, it evaluates the expression until value of *a* becomes *11* which means it evaluates loop ten times. What if the user has only 2 favourite foods? or the user have a list of his favourite foods which may be greater than 10. So in these types of cases we set a flag.

In the following code, first we set a flag equals to **True**. Then, we create empty list named it as *favourite_foods*. Then we use while loop. The loop will generate user defined input in each execution. Also we use **if statement** inside the **while loop**. If user gives input equals to full stop (.), then flag will set to **False** which means the loop will terminates. Otherwise, it will add another input to the list favourite foods

```
flag=True
favourite_foods=[]
while flag:
    user_input=input("Enter your favourite food: ")
    if user_input==".":
        flag=False
    else:
        favourite_foods.append(user_input)
```

Now again user gives names of two favourite foods i-e *Spaghetti Bolognese* and *Thai green curry*

Now user have only two favourite foods then he can terminate the while loop by giving input as full stop (.) as follows,

```
Enter your favourite food: Spaghetti Bolognese
Enter your favourite food: Thai green curry
```

Enter your favourite food:

```
.
```

By pressing enter the loop terminates. Now, we can check the items of list *favourite_foods* as follows,

```
favourite_foods
```

```
[' Spaghetti bolognese', 'Thai green curry']
```

In this loop users can give as many inputs as he wants. The loop will terminate when user wants to end.

Chapter 12

Changing Case

Python is case sensitive which means that if we take input from user and we don't define the user to use capital letter or small letter. For example,

If the person is applying to some driving job and he has to answer the following question,

```
Question=input("Do you have license?")
if Question =="YES":
    print("Congratulations!")
```

```
Do you have license?
yes
```

Here the user type yes, as yes is not to equals to YES in python so, it will not print "Congratulations!"

If we want to change the case of string data we can use the following built_in functions:

- upper()
- lower()
- title()

12.1 The function upper

In the following, we set a condition that if variable **Question** equals to **yes** than it must print "Congratulation!". Here we use function **upper()**. It basically returns the uppercased string from the given string. And if there is no lowercased character it will reture the original.

```
Question=input("Do you have license?")
if Question.upper() =="YES":
    print("Congratulations!")
```

```
Do you have license?yes
Congratulations!
```

Again, the user gives the input **yes**, the upper fuction will convert into **YES**.So YES equals to YES staisfy the condition will print "Congratulations!".

12.2 The function lower

Similarly, we can use **lower()** function. Here we assigned **CHAIR** to the variable **noun**. We convert it as follows,

```
noun="CHAIR"
noun.lower()
```

```
'chair'
```

12.3 The function title

This function will convert first letter of each word to upper case and remaining to the lower case. Here we want to change first alphabet of each word to upper case so we simply use function **title()**.

```
sen="you can do it"
sen.title()
```

```
'You Can Do It'
```

Great! We did it.

Task: Here we have a list *names.* Use this to complete task.

names = ["anna", "elsa", "trump"]

Run **for** loop that converts first letter of all the elements in the list to capital and displays each converted string.

Chapter 13

Functions

In python, the function is the way to achieve two things: Modularity and Reusability. Let's get familiar with these two:

1)Modularity: It means that we are breaking our programme into smaller and modular chunks. As our programme is not always simple but grows larger and larger, the function makes it organized and practicable.

2)Reusability: As word says it can be use again and again. So if we write multiple lines of code, we can give these lines a name and use these lines by just calling the name of function rather than writing the whole block of code again.

 **Key:** Rules for naming the function is same as naming the variable.

Syntax: We use the keyword **def** (for define) after that we will use function name with two parentheses **()**. We can also place input parameters or arguments within these parentheses or can also define parameters inside these parentheses followed by colon **(:)**

def function_name():

Here we define two variables *x* and *y.* We assign the value *5* to the variable *x* and *10* to the variable *y.* Also we have another variable *c* which add the values from *x* and *y* and store it as follows,

```
x=5
y=10
c=x+y
print(c)
```

15

We get the integer value *15* as an output. In the following topic, we will discuss that how we can do this by using functions.

13.1 Parameter less function

Function with no parameters within the parentheses of function definition.

13.1.1 User-defined functions

The function in which variables take the value from the user is called User-defined functions.

Here, we again define two variables *x* and *y*. Both variables take input from the user and convert the string data type to the integer data type.

And at last *print()* function will add these two variables and print their value.

```
x=int(input("Enter first value:"))
y=int(input("Enter second value:"))
print(x+y)
```

```
Enter first value:
|
```

Hint: Because of input function, programme flow will stop until the user gives the input.

Suppose, we assigned the values *5* and *10* to the variables *x* and *y* then it will print *15*.

Now if we want again to do this task we have to write it all over again.

We can do it again thousands times easily just by turning this code into function.

Here we defines the function named *add*.

```
def add():
    x=int(input("Enter first value:"))
    y=int(input("Enter second value:"))
    print(x+y)
```

By executing this block no operation will be performed. Function will not executes itself but remain in silent mode and didn't do anything until the function is called.

Remember: If we have a lot of functions in our programme .The programme will executes line by line but the interpreter will not enter in the body of the function.

For example, we have *print()* statement before and after the function.

By executing the following block we get output i-e *hye* and *bye*.

```
print("hye")
def body():
    print("You are here!")
print("bye")
```

```
hye
bye
```

But it didn't execute the function. It will execute only when it is called.

 Key: Two things matters

- function definition
- function call

That's how we call a function.

```
add()
```

```
Enter first value:
```

 Remember: The parentheses in the **function call** means to execute it. We can't get the value without using these parentheses in the call but get the function reference which points to some memory.

After enter the first value. It asks user for second input and it will give the output after adding these two numbers.

13.2 Parameterise function

Function with parameters within the parentheses of function definition.

13.2.1 Passing information positional argument

We learned that, how to make a function and code it. Suppose you made a function to subtract two values named the function as **subtract.** So whenever you call it by writing a **subtract()** it will execute the function robotically.

Now again look at this,

subtract()

Here we don't want these parentheses to be empty. We can put some information inside it. So whenever it executes, use these information .For example, we can write it as

subtract(10,5)

Now function will take these two values and subtract them. These values are called **arguments**. The arguments inside parentheses and separated by comma.

💡 **Key**: We can add as many arguments inside parentheses as we want, just separate them with a comma(,).

Syntax: First we have to write variables inside the function definition. These variables inside parentheses separated by comma **(,)**.We called these variables as parameters.

def function_name(parameter_1, parameter_2):

For example,

```
def subtract(a,b):
    print(a-b)
```

In the function **subtract ()** *a* and *b* are the parameters.

Here we call the function by passing the values **10** and **5**.And it will give the value of **5** after subtracting them

```
subtract(10,5)
```

 5

Note that the value **5** will assigned to the variable *a* and **10** to the variable *b*.

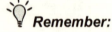
Now if we give arguments **1.5** and **5** then the result will be,

```
subtract(1.5,5)
```

 -3.5

As value **1.5** is assigned to *a* and **5** to *b*. As it subtract **5** from **1.5** i-e 1.5-5=-3.5

As, it display float value with the negative sign.

Here is another example,

```
def intro(name):
    print("My name is",name)
```

Now we call the function by passing the string.

```
intro("john")
```

```
My name is john
```

> ☀ **Remember:** If we pass argument greater or less then the parameter, we will get an error. So the number of argument must be equal to the number the parameters.

We call a function by passing the arguments to the function. They matched according to their position in the function call. In the following, we have a function *fullname* having three parameters: *first, Middle* and *last,*

```
def fullname(first,middle,last):
    print(first+middle+last)
```

```
fullname("Mohammad","Hamza","Iqbal")
```

```
MohammadHamzaIqbal
```

Here string *Mohammad* assigned to the *first*, *Hamza* assigned to *middle* and *Iqbal* assigned to the *last.*

> ☀ **Key:** The first argument will assign to first parameter similarly second will assigned to second parameter and so on. That's why they are known as positional arguments.

13.2.2 Passing information keyword argument

Another way of calling the function is by passing the argument as well as the parameter. By this method, position does not matter anymore but value (argument) will assigned to the matching variable in the function parameter.

Key: Sequence matters in positional arguments but not in the keyword argument.

Let's discuss the above example again, in which function *fullname* having three parameters: *first, Middle* and *last*. If we disturb the sequence, we will get different name. For example, if we pass middle name first and last name in the middle we will get,

```
fullname("Hamza","Iqbal","Mohammad")
```

HamzaIqbalMohammad

Now we will call the function again by passing the argument attach with the parameter. For example,

```
fullname(middle="Hamza",last="Iqbal",first="Mohammad")
```

MohammadHamzaIqbal

Note that there is no sequence in the arguments but we get the output orderly .Each value is assigned to their parameter by matching the keyword attached to it.

Middle value is assigned to the middle parameter although we pass this argument first but sequence does not matter anymore. Similarly, first value assigned to *first* parameter and value last to *last* parameter.

Now if we don't want to give all the keyword argument but only few one then we can write that parameter in the last. The Keyword **argument** always follows the positional argument. It can be written as follows,

```
fullname("Mohammad","Hamza",last="Iqbal")
```

MohammadHamzaIqbal

Now, if we pass the last keyword argument first, we will get an error as follows,

```
fullname(last="Iqbal","Mohammad","Hamza")
```

```
  File "<ipython-input-13-287bb79e6010>", line 1
    fullname(last="Iqbal","Mohammad","Hamza")
                         ^
SyntaxError: positional argument follows keyword argument
```

Also, if we do not know that how many arguments can a function take or how many arguments can a user pass? Then we will use **args**

13.2.3 Args

By this method, we can call a function by passing a various number of arguments. It is used to pass a non-keyword, variable-length argument list.

It uses the symbol **(*)**. Using this, the variable becomes iterable.

For example, if the user wants to pass more than one argument in the given parameter then it use * with the parameter. This parameter can store a lot of values inside it. As we read it before that a variable containing more values is known as **tuple.** So, when we get this parameter we see values store in the tuple.

We can write it as follows:

As this is known as optional number depends upon the user.

Here we have example of ordering pizza. As the function **_pizza_order_** have three main parameters i-e **size flavour** and **toppings**.

```
def pizza_order(size, flavor, toppings):
    print(f"Your {flavor} of size {size} having toppings of {toppings} is ready"
```

Now the restaurateur will take the order from customer by passing the arguments to the function like the following,

```
pizza_order(12,"BBQ Chicken Pizza","olives")
```
```
Your BBQ Chicken Pizza of size 12 having toppings of olives is ready
```

Now it prints the above message as an output. But, if the customer wants more than one topping?

We use * operation with the parameter topping. Now **_*toppings_** become the parameter deals with the arbitrary arguments. It can written as,

```
def pizza_order(size, flavor, *toppings):
    print(f"Your {flavor} of size {size} having toppings of {toppings} is ready"
```

Now we can pass more than one arguments for the parameter toppings as,

```
pizza_order(12,"BBQ Chicken Pizza","Olives","Mushrooms","Onions")
```

```
Your BBQ Chicken Pizza of size 12 having toppings of ('Olives', 'Mushrooms', 'O
nions') is ready
```

In output, note that all values in the last variable are in the form of tuple.

 Key: We always put arbitrary parameter in the last.

13.2.4 Default value parameter

We see that we call the parameterised function by passing the arguments.

If a user does not provide any arguments then type error will occur. To avoid any non deterministic behaviour python allows us to set default values in it. For example, we can set some default values as follows,

```
def add(x=2,y=3):
    print(x+y)
```

As parameter **x** having default value of **2** and **y** having value of **3**.Now we call it without passing the arguments so the output will be,

```
add()
```

```
5
```

As the function uses it default values and print something. If the user just passes the argument **y** then we will get,

```
add(y=7)
```

9

As the user do not pass **x** so the function use default value of **x** but update the value of **y** with **7** so it prints **9.**

Looking again to the previous example of the function **_fullname_**. This function takes three arguments and assigned to their respective parameters. Let's suppose a person have no middle name. Now we can set default value of the middle name. So if the user doesn't enters its middle name the default value will print.

Remember: Like the keyword arguments, if we only want some parameter set as default so the default arguments should follows the non_default arguments in the function definition like,

_def fun(non_default,default=2)_

```
def fullname(first,last,middle=" "):
    print(first+middle+last)
```

Here we put default value of space in argument middle. So when user don't have middle name the function will use space bar.

Now user calls the function by passing its name consist of first name and last name as follows:

```
fullname("David","Smith")
```

David Smith

As it use the default value i-e space instead of making an error.

13.2.5 Passing information back from them

When we call a function then function will perform the task given to it. The function receives values, processes it and prints it.

For example, we have a function *add* .Now we call this function by passing the arguments and the function prints integer *18* by processing it as follows,

```
def add(x,y):
    c=x+y
    print(c)
add(9,9)
```

18

Now, we want to do some operations with the result of the function but unfortunately, we cannot do it because the result still present inside the body of the function. As, the value of *c* print on screen but it is not possible for us to use it

Now to take out this value we use keyword **return()**. These returned values can be assign, reuse and modify then.

We write return inside the body of function. We can code it as follows,

```
def add(x,y):
    c=x+y
    return c
result=add(9,9)
```

Now this returned the value inside the variable *c* to the variable result which is outside the body.

- First we call the function by passing arguments.
- The values are assigned to the variable *x* and *y*.
- The result of adding these values is assigned to the variable *c*.
- Keyword return will give value of *c* to the variable *result* outside the function body.

Key: The value of variable result is replaced by *c*. Now whatever will be in *c* assigned to variable *result* i-e add(9,9) is replaced by variable *c*.

We will re-utilize this value anytime. For example,

```
result*2
```

36

We multiplied result with *2* then we get integer value *36*.i-e as result having value of *36*.

13.2.6 Return multiple values

We can also return more than one value at a time. It can be

- String
- Float

- Integer
- Any user defined input.

  For example,

```
def add(x,y):
    c=x+y
    return 'hello!',c
result=add(9,9)
```

As it return string value **hello** as well as the variable **c**. Now let's see what we have in the result.

```
print(result)
```

```
('hello!', 18)
```

First it prints the string value after that it prints the value of the variable **c**.

Now see another example. Here we have a function **intro** having two parameters **h1** and **h2**. Here **h1** means the number of houses in California and **h2** refers to the number of houses in New York.

```
def intro(h1,h2):
    h=h1+h2
    print(h)
    return'hello!',input("enter your name:"),f"you are owner of {h} houses"
```

Here keyword **return()** returns multiple values

- First it returns the string "hello!". After that, it takes the input from user and at last it return message.
- Now we call the function by passing arguments.

Remember that the number of arguments must be equal to the number of parameters.

Let's suppose the person having 2 houses in California and 1 in New York then user can call function as:

```
intro(2,1)
```
```
enter your name: |
```

Next, Python display a box, which represent user defined value so it needs the input from user to print full message. Here user enters the name **John**. Now it prints the following output.

```
('hello!', 'John', 'you are owner of 3 houses')
```

 Remember:

If we enter anything after return statement inside the body of a function, it will never print because that line will never executes.

Here the print statement having string value the end never executes.

```
def intro(a,b):
    c=a+b
    return c
    print("the end")
```

Return must be the last line of execution in the function.

If we want to print this message we can take this statement out of the body by removing the indentation.

The statement return [expression] exits a function, optionally passing back an expression to the caller. A return statement with no arguments is the same as return **None.**

13.3 Using function as variables

Basically, the main purpose of function is that it can be use as the variables. This is done by calling the function in the expression.

Here we have two different functions *mul* and *div.* These functions having parameters *a* and *b* .We can assign different values to the argument of two functions.

```
def mul(a,b):
    result=a*b
    return result
def div(a,b):
    result=a/b
    return result
```

Now, we call these functions inside the new variable *c*. It will perform addition and assign the result to the variable *c.*

```
c=mul(5,10)+div(6,3)
```

- First, the function *div* call and assign arguments *6* and *3* to parameters *a* and *b*.
- Now it divides *a* by *b* and returns the result to *div(6,3)*
- Similarly, second function called by passing the arguments *5* and *10* to the variable *a* and *b*.
- Now values of *a* and *b* will updated from *6* and *3* to *5* and *10*

> **Key:** We can also use different parameters in function *mul* instead of *a* and *b.*

After that it will multiply both and assign the result to *mul(5,10).*

Now both values will add and gives us the following output,

139

```
print(c)
```
52.0

13.3.1 Local and global variables

Let's discuss two types of variable used in the functions.

13.3.1.1 Local variable

Local variables are the variables, which defines inside the body of the function.

The scope is only inside the function as it means that they are recognized locally. They are not accessible outside the function.

We have a function *yesterday* in the following code,

```
def yesterday():
    weather="Sunny"
    print(f"Yesterday was {weather}")
```

Look there is a variable *weather* inside the function body. So it is local variable .String *Sunny* is stored in this local variable. When we call the function *yesterday* we get the following output,

```
yesterday()
```

```
Yesterday was Sunny
```

As we studied that local variable are not able to access from outside the body. So, if want to access the local variable *weather* it will produce an error.

```
weather
```

```
---------------------------------------------------------------
--
NameError                                Traceback (most recent call las
t)
<ipython-input-19-580cf3bfbc8a> in <module>
----> 1 weather

NameError: name 'weather' is not defined
```

It says that the variable **weather** is not defined.

13.3.1.2 Global variable

Global variables are the variables, which defines outside the body of the function.

Global scope is like global fame as these can be accessed and modify from inside as well outside the function.

Again, we have the function *today*. Now we have a variable *weather2* in which string *Rainy* is stored. The variable *weather2* is outside the function so it is global variable. Inside the function there is print statement, which prints the value of a global variable successfully.

```
weather2="Rainy"
def today():
    print(f"today is {weather2} day")
```

If we call the function *today*, it will print the following message,

```
today()
```
today is Sunny day

Now as **weather2** is global variable so it should be accessible from outside the body of function like,

```
weather2
```
'Sunny'

Great! it prints the string value stored in it.

13.4 Function within function

Till now we have learnt how to make the function. Now we can also call the function within the other function.

- Suppose we have a function name **commission_calculator** in which we set different conditions. We have given parameter **sales** to the function **commission_calculator**.

- We use **if statement** for decision making. It will run throughout the body and check the condition. It returns when the condition is true.

- Another function is **salary_calculator.** This function has two parameters i-e **basic** and **sales**.

- Inside the function we have a variable **grossSalary** which adds two parameters i-e **basic** and **sales** (from the first function **commission_calculator**). It can code as follows,

```
def commission_calculator(sales):
    if sales>100:
        return sales*100
    elif sales>50:
        return sales*50
    elif sales>20:
        return sales*20
    else:
        return 0
def salary_calculator(basic,sales):
    grossSalary=basic+commission_calculator(sales)
    print(f"Your gross salary is {grossSalary}")
```

Now we have to call the main function *salary_calculator* by passing the arguments. Here the data type of both arguments will be integer. We call the function by passing the values *500* as *basic* and *55* as *sales*

```
salary_calculator(500,55)
```

```
Your gross salary is 3250
```

- First, by calling the function it assigned the values of arguments in their parameter.

- The integer *500* assigned to parameter basic and integer *55* assigned to parameter s*ales*. Sales called in the function *commission_calcutor.*

- Now *commission_calculator* check all condition. As, sales is not greater than *100* so it check next condition. The next condition says that the sale must be greater than *50* as sales equals to *55* which is greater than *50* so condition is true.

- Then, it returned the value by multiplying sales with *50 i-e 50*50 equals to 2750*

- The variable *grossSalary* adds basic and sales i-e 500+2750 equals to 3250.

- Then print the following output,

  "Your gross salary is 3250"

Task: Code a function *full_name* having two parameters (first_name and last_name). Concatenate *first_name* and *last_name* and assigns the result to a variable *x,* and passes the result back to the calling code.

Chapter 14

Classes

14.1 Introduction

As Python is an object oriented programming language. It means all the code in python is implemented using special construct called **class.**

The first concept of object oriented programming language is classes.

A class is defined as a model, blueprint(map) of anything or it is also defined as something that can be followed to create objects and instances.

In Python, **classes** are template. Template means that we can create similar things by using that template. For example, when someone conduct a survey of the questionnaire sort, he hands you a survey form having some listed questions in it. Surveyor asked Surveye, to answer all the questions written in the form. *Why doesn't the surveyor gives you a blank sheet and asked to write your thoughts on that specific topic?* As the survey team wants only specific information about that subject from you. The form is just like a template that makes things easier for both surveyor and the surveyee. It organized information so that the result is easily concluded from that specific set of information.

The advantage of using classes is to keep related things together.

Syntax: Python use keyword **class** to define a class. And write name of class with parenthesis and colon **(:)**

class Survey() :

#body of class

After colon body of a class starts. Now we might think that what class holds inside its body? So a class can hold two things:

- A class may hold attributes
- A class may hold behaviours

In programming, attributes means **variables** and behaviours means **functions**.

We will discuss both variable and function within the class one by one

Looking to the example of class. Let's talk about some real example such as car. We all are familiar with common attributes of a car such as color of a car, size of a car, model of a car or setting capacity of a car. Similarly, we also notice some behaviours of a car which includes movement of a car, acceleration of a car, deceleration of a car or steering speed of a car. These are called functions of class car.

Here we write a class named *Car*,

class Car() :

#body of class

#attributes and behaviours

Here the car company can store information of different cars but all the information is to be structured in the same way.

14.2 Variable in the class

In class first we have to define the attributes/variables. Those attributes must be in object of that specific class.

Syntax:

For that we make a function by using,

- keyword **def**.
- After that we type underscore two time (__)
- Then type keyword **init**
- Again, type two times underscore (__)
- Opening the parentheses, then write keyword **self** as first parameter
- After that we can write attributes of that class
- End the line with closing parentheses and colon (:)
  For example,

```
class Car():
    def __init__(self,color):
```

Here we have a class **Car()**. Now we have to define the attribute of class *Car* i-e color.

After that we must have a variable having same value as attributes

```
class Car():
    def __init__(self,color):
        self.car_color=color
```

Note that second line is intended because of colon in the end of first line which means second line is in the body of a class.

Inside the function body, we write variables. Here we declare a variable *self.car_color* in which we save the value of the attribute *color*.

Note that third line in the above code is more intended than second line.

We can also defined attributes of a class before as the following

class Car() :

#class attributes

type= "Toyota"

def__init__(self,attribute):

#instance attributes

self.attribute=attribute

14.3 Objects

Almost everything in Python is an object with its properties and methods.

Objects are instances of classes. All objects follow the specific class.

We defined the class above named it as **Car().** By defining it, means we only defined the description of object.

> **Information**: No memory or storage is allocated by just defining the class.

Object are made following its class, means that object belongs to a class. The instances must have been following the requirements set by the class.

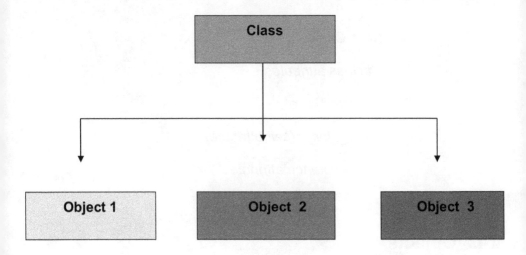

Syntax:

First we write name of object, then assignment operator **(=)**, then name of a class and parenthesis **()**.

object1 = Class()

Similarly, for creating **object 2** we can write the following,

object2 = Class()

💡 **Knowledge**: We can create as many objects as we want for a specific class.

14.3.1 Creating objects for class

We defined a class **car()** above .Now we have to create objects for that class.

In the following line, we create first object **car1**.

```
car1=Car("black")
```

Here we assigned the string "black" to the class attribute **color.**

Knowledge: As we write ,

car1=car("black")

It's mean that we are creating a copy (instance) of a class **car ()** having a unique identifier **car1**, and fill the information of the attribute **color** with the name of the for this particular color i-e **black.**

Similarly, we create second object **car2** as follows,

```
car2=Car("red")
```

Now we don't need to tell Python that where this string **red** to be stored because at this stage the class **Car** has only one attribute i-e **color.**

Knowledge: It works like positional arguments.

14.3.2 Multiple attributes

Now if we don't have a simple class but a little more complex as it has more than one attribute. Re-calling the previous example in which we created the class **Car()** having only one attribute i-e **color**. Now adding more attributes like make and model of a car to it.

Remember: Each attribute is separated by comma.

We can code this as follows,

```
class Car():
        def __init__(self,color,make,model):
```

Again, we declare three different variable which having same values as attributes of the class. All these starts with first parameter i-e *self* followed by a dot (.) as follows,

```
class Car():
    def __init__(self,color,make,model):
        self.car_color=color
        self.car_make=make
        self.car_model=model
```

Remember: All the rules of naming variables are also implementing for naming a class name.

Now, Class *Car* having three different attributes i-e *color, make* and *model*. It means each object of instance must have values for these three attributes: **color, make and model.**

Knowledge: We can write any name for the first parameter instead of self. The purpose of first parameter is to make individual copies of each instances so that the information do not over write.

Now, we can get a better idea by looking to the following diagram,

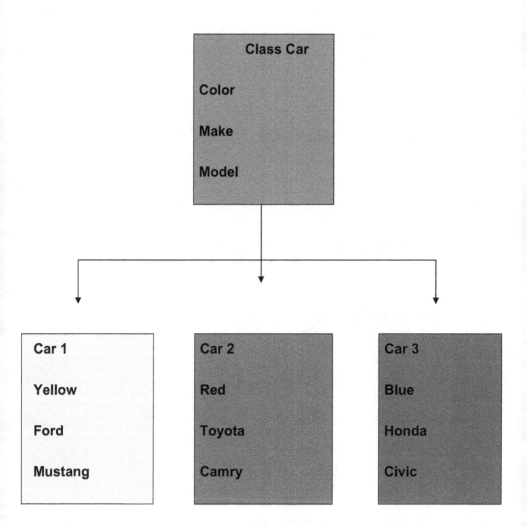

The class *Car()* have three instances i-e *Car 1* , *Car 2* and *Car 3*. These instances are fulfilling the properties of a class **car**. In the instance we provide all the mandatory properties (in the initialization).

Now we code to create instance *Car_1* having string values "Yellow", "Ford" and "Mustang" in it. We can write it as follows,

```
Car_1=Car("Yellow","Ford","Mustang")
```

Now new instance must have unique name not similar to the first instance i-e *Car_1*

Here we have instance *Car_2* holding string values in it.

```
Car2=Car("Red","Toyota","Camry")
```

Similarly, another instance *Car_3* having different string values as,

```
Car_3=Car("Blue","Honda","Civic")
```

Note that in each instance, there's a value that matches up with the

attribute, in the class definition above.

Instance *Car_1* first create copy of the class. After that it matches its values with the attributes of a class. As the string value *Yellow* matches up with class attribute *color*, *Ford* matches up with attribute *make* and *Mustang* matches up with attribute *model*.

The instance *Car_2* creates new copy of a class. The string value *Red* matches up with class attribute *color*, *Toyota* matches up with

attribute *make* and *Camry* matches up with attribute *model*

Similarly, instance *Car_3* also works same as instances *Car_1* and

Car_2.

Hint:

Python matches the string values of instance with the attribute of the

class according to their order. Classes and instance are like functions

and function call i-e the arguments in the function call matches up with

the parameter in the function.

14.3.3 Building functions within the classes

Recalling the previous example, we have a class name *Car.* This class

has three attributes: *color, make* and *model*. Each instance of the class

Car contains values that match these attributes. Let's add one more

attribute to the class to make little more complex.

```python
class Car():
        def __init__(self, color, make, model,price):
            self.car_color=color
            self.car_make=make
            self.car_model=model
            self.car_price=price
```

Also, we have other variable having same value of attribute i-e *price.*

Now here we will discuss about building a function within the class. The function will able to return full description of that instance. For example, to get the information of instances of **Car, w**e write the function as follows,

```
class Car():
    def _init_(self, color, make, model,price):
        self.car_color=color
        self.car_make=make
        self.car_model=model
        self.car_price=price

    def description_of_car(self):
        print(f"The starting price of {self.car_make} model {self.car_model} having color {self.car_color}is ${self.car_price}")
```

14.3.3.1 Calling a function

Now we check it by calling the function. First write instance name followed by a dot **(.)** then write the function name with parenthesis **()**

instance_name.function_name()

For instance **Car_1,** the function shows the following output,

```
Car_1.description_of_car()
```

```
The starting price of Ford model Mustang having
color Yellowis $35630
```

Also, we can also define more function to this class

All the attributes and behaviours are available for each instance. We also can check it. For example, again calling the function *description_of_car* for the instance *Car_2*

```
Car_2.description_of_car()
```

The starting price of Toyota model Camry having
color Red is $35130

As it don't over write the value of instance *Car_1* but having individual copies of the function *description_of_car* for instance *Car_2.*

Hint: You can check available variable and function for that instance by first writing the name of that instance followed by dot and then pressing the tab.

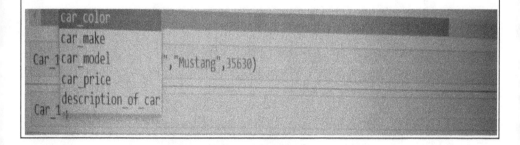

Here the available variables are *car_color, car_make, car_model* and *car_price* whereas we have only one function in the class i-e *description_of_car.*

We use first parameter i-e *self* to access any attributes of a class

Now we build another function **budget()**. In this function we set a condition that if the price of car is less than or equal to 36000 then it shows the output *"Great! This car price is in your budget."*

We write the following code inside class **Car()**

```
def budget(self):
    if self.price<=36000:
        print("Great!This car price is in your budget")
```

As the values of instance **Car_1** are as follows,

```
Car_1=Car("Yellow","Ford","Mustang",35630)
```

Now we call a function **budget()**,

```
Car_1.budget()
```

```
Great!This car price is in your budget
```

As it shows the output because $35630 is less than $36000

Task: Build a class named it as employee, having five attributes Name, Age, Gender, Id and Department. Also build a function inside a class name it as role of employee.(Hint: for building a function revise the chapter)

14.3.4 Accessing values from the instance

Till now we created three instances *Car_1, Car_2, Car_3* of a class *Car*.

The instances had three values in them. These values matched with the attributes of a class i-e color of a car ,make of a car and model of a car.

Now if we want to get information from instances we can get it easily.

Syntax:

- First write name of unique identifier of the instance. For the above example the identifier of instances are *Car_1, Car_2* and *Car_3*
- Then write dot (.)
- At last write name of attribute which we want to display.

indentifier.attribute

If we want to get *color* of *Car_1* we write the following code:

```
Car_1.car_color
```
```
'Yellow'
```

Now, if we want to know about the *make* of *Car_2* we write,

```
Car_2.car_make
```
```
'Toyota'
```

Similarly, we write the following code to get information about *model* of *Car_3* we write the code as follows,

```
Car_3.car_model
```

'Civic'

Great! We got the information out of instances.

14.3.5 Adding an attribute value to a class

As we have a class *car()* having attributes *color, make, model* and *price*. Also we have three instances *Car_1*, *Car_2* and *Car_3*. Now we want to add a new attribute *GPS_Navigation_System* to the instance *Car_1*. We can add it by using function *setattr()*

In this function, first we pass instance name then name of the attribute and at last, value of that attribute. We can write it as follows,

```
setattr(Car_1,'GPS_Navigation_System','yes')
```

Knowledge: If the attribute already exists then the function *setattr()* set the value of that attribute.

Now, we access that attribute with the function *getattr()*. In this function first we pass the instance name than the name of attribute as in the following code,

```
getattr(Car_1,'GPS_Navigation_System')
```

'yes'

Remember: The attribute name should be in commas.

The value of the attribute is only added to the instance *Car_1*.If we want to get this attribute for other instance like *Car_2* and *Car_3* it will shows us an error.

```
Car_2.GPS_Navigation_System
```

```
------------------------------------------------------------------
----------
AttributeError                          Traceback (most recent c
all last)
<ipython-input-218-90ca7cfdc2bd> in <module>
----> 1 Car_2.GPS_Navigation_System

AttributeError: 'Car' object has no attribute 'GPS_Navigation_Syst
em'
```

14.3.6 Deleting an attribute value of a class

We can also delete any specific attribute from the instance by using function *delattr()*. First we have to pass instance name and then the attribute name which we have to delete. Now we want to delete the attribute price from instance Car_1. We can write the code as follows,

```
delattr(Car_1,'price')
```

It removes the attribute price from instance *Car_1* but still it is present in other instances *Car_2* and *Car_3*

14.3.7 Checking an attribute value of a class

To check the attribute weather it is present in the instance or not, we simply use the function *hasattr()*. This function also needs the instance name and the attribute name which have to be check. Now we want to see that the attribute *GPS_Naviagtion_System* is present in the instance *Car_1* so we write the following code,

```
hasattr(Car_1,'GPS_Navigation_System')
```

True

It returns **True**. As the instance **Car_2** doesn't has this attribute so when we check for **Car_2** it would returns **False**.

```
hasattr(Car_2,'GPS_Navigation_System')
```

False

14.3.8 Changing an attribute value of a class

First write name of the instance followed by dot(.). Then write the attribute which we want to update. And then assign new value to it by writing new value after assignment operator,

instance_name.attribute=new_value

Again recalling the previous example, we defined a class **Car()** having three instances **Car_1, Car_2** and **Car_3.**

Also, we know that we can easily get all the information out of these instances .Here we get the value for attribute **color** of instance **Car_1** by writing the following code,

```
Car_1.car_color
```

'Yellow'

Now we want to change the color for instance **Car_1** from **Yellow** to **Black** we can write it as follows

```
Car_1.car_color="Black"
```

We can verify it by calling the attribute through instance. As,

```
Car_1.car_color
```

```
'Black'
```

Great! Value updated.

14.3.9 Default attributes

We can also set a default attribute in the class. Default attribute is the one which don't pass in the constructor. For example in the class *Car* we set default variable battery. Here is the code,

```
class Car():
    def __init__(self, color, make, model):
            self.car_color=color
            self.car_make=make
            self.car_model=model
            self.battery="300 amp"
```

Note that attribute *battery* is not coming through the construction *init* like other attributes *color ,make* and *model*

Now we build a function *battery* related to this attribute in the following block,

```
class Car():
    def __init__(self, color, make, model):
        self.car_color=color
        self.car_make=make
        self.car_model=model
        self.battery="300 amp"
    def battery(self):
        print(f"The battery of the car is{self.battery}")
```

Now if we call this function for instance *Car_1* the output will be,

```
Car_1.battery
```

```
'300 amp'
```

Similarly, the output will be same for other instances *Car_2* and *Car_3.*
We can check it as follows,

```
Car_2.battery
```

```
'300 amp'
```

```
Car_3.battery
```

```
'300 amp'
```

Now if we want to change the values of the battery for each car we can update the values.

We can change the attribute value by two ways

- By direct hitting the value

- Via a function(get set)

First we do the *hitting the value* method. Like for instance **Car_1** the battery should be of **440 amp** so we can amend it as follows,

```
Car_1.battery="440 amp"
```

Now for instance **Car_2** we changed the value of battery from **300 amp** to **770 amp**

```
Car_2.battery="770 amp"
```

Similarly, for instance **Car_3** we change the value of battery to **410 amp** as follows,

```
Car_3.battery="410 amp"
```

Now all the values of attribute **battery** are updated. We can check it for instance **Car_1** as follows,

```
Car_1.battery
```

```
'440 amp'
```

For **Car_2,**

```
Car_2.battery
```

```
'770 amp'
```

Similarly for **Car_3** we will get,

```
Car_3.battery
```

```
'410 amp'
```

In this method we are hitting the attribute battery directly by instances *Car_1, Car_2* and *Car_3* which is not an appropriate method.

We can do this by defining a function inside the class *Car*.

Here we build a new function having parameter *self*. In this function, we are setting size so we added new parameter *new_size.* The function *set_battery_size()* can be written as follows,

```
def set_battery_size(self,new_size):
        self.battery=new_size
```

Also we want to get new battery size. For that we build another function *get_battery_size()*.

```
def get_battery_size(self):
        print(f"The size of your's car battery is {self.battery}")
```

As in the above function we don't need any argument so we only have one parameter *self* in it.

Let's think that we have the *battery_size* equals to **300 amp** for all three instances *Car_1,Car_2* and *Car_3*.

Now we update this value by using the function *set_battery_size()*.
Note, that this function has a parameter *new_size,* so we call this
function by passing the argument.

```
Car_1.set_battery_size("440 amp")
```

Similarly, we update values of attribute *battery* of remaining instances
Car_2 and *Car_3* by the following code,

```
Car_2.set_battery_size("770 amp")
Car_3.set_battery_size("410 amp")
```

Check the updated values by calling the function *get_battery_size()*

First, we will check the value of instance *Car_1(),*

```
Car_1.get_battery_size()
```
```
The size of your's car battery is 440 amp
```

Now checking the value of attribute battery for instance *Car_2,*

```
Car_2.get_battery_size()
```
```
The size of your's car battery is 770 amp
```

Similarly for instance *Car_3* we write as follows,

```
Car_3.get_battery_size()
```
```
The size of your's car battery is 410 amp
```

Great! Now we get all updated values

Task:

Make a class of student having attributes **first_name, last_name, percentage** and **grade**. Inside a class build a function **promoted**. In function set a condition if grades are equal or greater than 70 percentage then output message would be (f "{self.first_Name} {self.last_name} is promoted to {self.grade})

Hint The variable *self.grade* must be equal to grade incremented by 1 i-e *self.grade=grade+1*

14.4 Class Inheritance

We can create more classes by using original class instead of starting from scratch, by using the concept of Inheritance. Inheritance is a method of creating new classes by using the details of existing class without changing it.

Now here we have two types of classes,

- **Original class:** The original or existing class is called base class.
- **New class:** The class which inherits the property of the base class is called derived class.

> **Knowledge**: Base class is also known as parent class or super class and derived class is also called child class or sub class

We have following types of Inheritance:

- Single Inheritance

- Multiple Inheritance
- Multi level Inheritance
- Hierarchical Inheritance
- Hybrid Inheritance

  We will discuss each one by one.

14.4.1 Single Inheritance

Single Inheritance means that **a derived class** inherits the method and attributes from single base class.

Syntax: First, we have to write the base class and after that we define derived class. We use keyword class to define both classes,

class Base_Class:

body of base class

class Dervied_Class(Base_Class):

body of derived class

In the following diagram, Classes are represented as boxes. The inheritance relationship is represented by an arrow from base class pointing to the derived class,

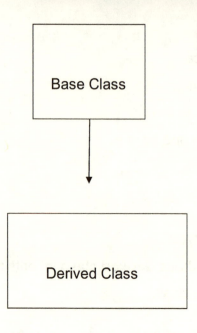

Base Class

Derived Class

Let's do an example of Inheritance. Recalling the above example of class *Car*(). Here we have super class *Vehicle()* and a sub class *Car()*.

First, we define the super class *Vehical()* as follows,

```
class Vehicle:
    def __init__(self, make, color):
        self.make = make
        self.color = color

    def get_make(self):
        return self.make
```

In the super class *Vehicle(),* we instantiate a constructor with *make* and *color*.

After super class, we define the sub class *Car().* In the parentheses we put the name of the parent class i-e *Vehicle.*

We write the code for sub class as follows,

```
class Car(Vehicle):

    def __init__(self, make, model, color):
        super().__init__(make, color)
        self.model = model

    def get_description(self):
        return "The car is " + self.color +" "+ self.make +" "+ self.model
```

Here, we call the constructor from the sub class Car using **super()**. Also we created a **get_description** method which is returning **self.model** from sub class. Also this method is returning **self.make, self.color** from the super class **Vehicle()**.

Hint: We call the attributes from super class by using **super()**. Super() allows us to call a method from the base (super) class. We can also use name of the super class instead of super().

Now, we define instance **c** for sub class **Car()**. As the string values matches with the attribute of class,

```
c = Car("Ford",  "Mustang", " Yellow")
print("Car description:", c.get_description())
print(c.get_make())
```

```
Car description: The car is  Yellow Ford Mustang
Ford
```

Here the string value **Ford** assigned to **make, Mustang** assigned to **model** and **Yellow** assigned to **color.**

Note that above block have two print statements. In the first print statement we call the method **get_description** from the sub class **Car()**.

And in the second print statement we call the method ***get_make*** from the super *class()*

14.4.2 Multiple Inheritance

In Inheritance we see that a derived class inherits the method and attributes from base class. If the derived class inherits the property from multiple base classes then it is known as multiple inheritance.

This method allows us to use the properties from multiple base classes in a derived or child class.

Syntax:

> *class Base_Class_1:*
>
> > *body of base class*
>
> *class Base_Class_2:*
>
> > *body of base class*
>
> *class Dervied_Class(Base_Class_1,Base_Class_2):*
>
> > *body of derived class*

In the following diagram, the inheritance relationship is represented by an arrow from two base classes pointing to the same derived class.

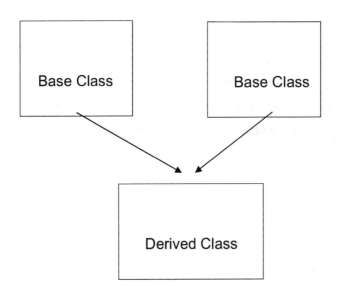

Recalling the above example, where we have a super class **Vehicle()** having a sub class **Car().** Now we do the same example with the concept of multiple inheritance. Here we have super class having attribute **make** as follows,

```
class Vehicle:
    def __init__(self, make):
        self.make = make
    def get_brand_name(self):
        return self.make
```

Now we add another super class **Cost()** having attribute **cost,** as in the following,

```
class Cost:
    def __init__(self, cost):
        self.cost = cost
    def get_cost(self):
        return self.cost
```

So here we have sub class **Car**. It works similar to the inheritance example discussed previous. We have created a **get_description** method which is returning **self.model** from sub class. Also this method is returning **self.make** and **self.cost** from the super classes **Vehicle()** and **Cost()**

```
class Car(Vehicle, Cost):
    def __init__(self, make, model, cost):
        self.model = model
        Vehicle.__init__(self, make)
        Cost.__init__(self, cost)
    def get_description(self):
        return "The starting price of "+self.make+self.model + " is $ " + self.get_cost()
```

Note that,

- We want to inherit the properties of both super classes **Vehicle** and **Cost**. So, we have to write the name of super class inside the parenthesis of sub class.
- We call the attribute in the constructor of sub class **Car** by using another method i-e the name of super class,

    Vehicle.__init__(self,make)

    Cost.__init__(self,cost)

Now we define instances **c** of sub class **Car** as follows,

```
c = Car("Ford ",  "Mustang", "35630")
print("Car description:", c.get_description())
```

Car description: The starting price of Ford Mustang is
$ 35630

The values match with the attributes. Here string value **Ford** matches
with **self.make, Mustang** matches with **self.model** and **$35630**
matches with the attribute **cost.**

14.4.3 Multilevel Inheritance

In multilevel inheritance, we have one base class, one derived class and
sub derived class which means that the feature of base class and
derived class is further inherited by another derived class.

Snytax:

class Base_Class:

body of base class

class Derived_Class(Base_Class):

body of derived class

class Dervied_Class_2(Derived_Class):

body of derived class

In the following diagram, Classes are represented as boxes. The
inheritance relationship is represented by an arrow from the base class
pointing to the derived class. And another, derived class is inherited from
derived class.

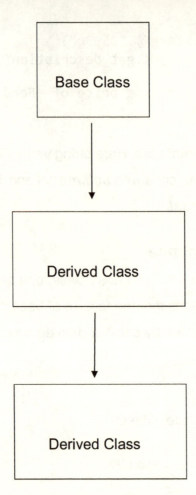

This type of Inheritance works same as relationship between child and grandfather. Let's do an example. We can write the following code to define a base class named *Grandfather()*

```
class Grandfather:
    grandfathername =None
    def grandfather(self):
        print(self.grandfathername)
```

Also we derived a class from a base class named *Father()*.

```
class Father(Grandfather):
    fathername = None
    def father(self):
        print(self.fathername)
```

Now we define another class which is further derived from class **Father()**

```
class Son(Father):
    def parent(self):
        print("My Grandfather name is", self.grandfathername)
        print("And my Father name is", self.fathername)
```

Now we define instances **s** for the class **Son()**. First we are assigning string values **Graham** and **John** to the variables **grandfathername** and **fathername**. Then we are calling method parent from the derived class **Son()**.

```
s = Son()
s.grandfathername = "Graham"
s.fathername = "John"
s.parent()
```

By running above code we get the following output,

```
My Grandfather name is Graham
And my Father name is John
```

Task: Define a class *student()* with one attribute *major* and one method. The method displays the attribute. Code an instance of the class and call the method.

14.4.4 Hierarchical Inheritance

This type of Inheritance is achieved when we have only one base class and we created multiple derived classes using that single base. The feature of base class is inherited by multiple derived classes.

Syntax:

class Base_Class:

body of base class

class Derived_Class_1(Base_Class):

body of derived class

class Dervied_Class_2(Base_Class):

body of derived class

In the following diagram, Classes are represented as boxes. The inheritance relationship is represented by an arrow from the base class pointing to two different derived classes.

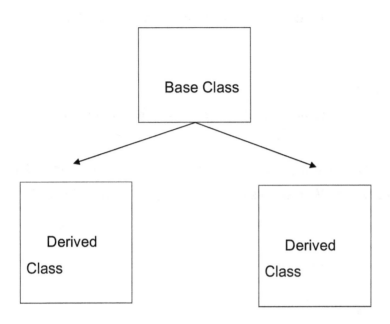

Recalling the above example, Now we have a base class named **Father().** Inside it we assign a keyword **None** to it. Also we have a method **def father** inside the body of a class as following,

```
class Father:
    fathername =None
    def father(self):
        print(self.fathername)
```

Now we have a derived class named **Son_1().** In this class, we have a method **parent().** Inside the function **parent()** we also write print statement which returning value of **self.fathername.**

```
class Son_1(Father):
    def parent(self):
        print(f"My name is Jac and my father name is {self.fathername}")
```

We have another derived class **Son_2** of the base class as follows,

```
class Son_2(Father):
    def parent(self):
        print(f"My name is Jerry and my father name is {self.fathername}")
```

Now we define two instances, **s1** for the derived class **Son_1** and **s2** for derived class **Son_2**. We also assigned string value **Ben** to the variable **fathername.**

```
s1 = Son_1()
s2 = Son_2()
s1.fathername = "Ben"
s2.fathername = "Ben"
```

Note that we assigned values for both instances **s1** and **s2.**

We get the following output by calling the method **parent()** from the derived class **Son_1** and **Son_2.**

```
s1.parent()
s2.parent()
```

```
My name is Jac and my father name is Ben
My name is Jerry and my father name is Ben
```

Let's do another example. We have a super class named as **Pologon ().** As polygon has common features width and height so, we define the both variable and initialize them with keyword **None** in class.

In the super class we also define a function **set_values** and use the method to set the values of both variables. Also this method will take two arguments i-e length and width.

def set_values (self ,length ,width)

We cannot inherit the private members of super class to sub class. As both the variables **__length** and **__width** are private members of class **Polygon**. This is called encapsulation. We will study it in detail in the next section

Hint: We use double underscore (__) to make a variable private.

So to access private members we use **get()** method. We can write it as the following code,

```
class Polygon:
    __width=None
    __height=None

    def set_values(self,width,height):
        self.__width=width
        self.__height=height
    def get_width(self):
        return self.__width
    def get_height(self):
        return self.__height
```

Also, we have sub classes **Rectangle** and **Triangle**. So they can inherit some properties from super class **Polygon.**

Now, we define a sub class **Rectangle** which is having a function **area()**. As rectangle area is obtain by multiplying its length and its width. We write it as follows,

Hint: The subclass is not intended as compared to super class.

```
class Rectangle(Polygon):
    def area(self):
        return self.get_width()*self.get_height()
```

Remember: To inherit the properties of super class, we have to write the name of super class inside the parenthesis of sub class.

Also we define another sub class **Triangle** having a function **area()** and we know that triangle area is obtain by its multiplying length with its width and dividing the product with **2**. We defined it the class as follows,

```
class Triangle(Polygon):
    def area(self):
        return self.get_width()*self.get_height()/2
```

Hint: When you use inheritance, a relation **is a** is built between Base class and derived class. In above example **Rectangle is a Polygon**. Also, **Triangle is a Polygon.**

Now we define the instance **Rec** of the subclass **Rectangle()**

and instance **Tri** of subclass **Triangle().**

So, we call the function by passing two arguments i-e width and length as follows,

```
Rec=Rectangle()
Tri=Triangle()
Rec.set_values(3,5)
Tri.set_values(3,5)
print(Rec.area())
print(Tri.area())
```

```
15
7.5
```

So these integer values *3* and *5* are assigned to the **width** and **height** of rectangle. So, it returns the product to **15** to the **area**.

Also, we pass same value for triangle. The integer *3* and *5* again assigned to **width** and **height** of **triangle**. It returns the value by multiplying *3* and *5* and dividing the answer by *2* which gives us *7.5*

Note that we don't define the function **set_value** inside the sub class **Rectangle** and **Triangle** but as they are inheriting from the **Polygon** class. So it can also use the members of the **Polygon.**

14.4.5 Hybrid Inheritance

Hybrid Inheritance consists of multiple types of inheritances.

Knowledge: It may be combination of multiple inheritance and multilevel inheritance.

Syntax:

class Base_Class:

    body of base class

class Derived_Class_1(Base_Class):

    body of derived class

class Dervied_Class_2(Base_Class):

    body of derived class

class Derived_Class_3(Derived_Class_1,Derived_Class_2)

    body of derived class

In the following diagram, Classes are represented as boxes. The inheritance relationship is represented by an arrow from the base class pointing to the two different derived classes. And another, derived class is inherited from these two derived classes.

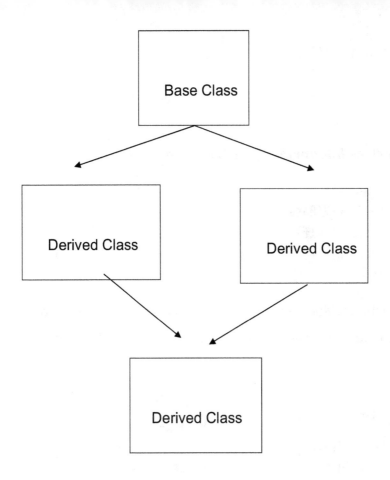

So in the following block we have a base class named it as **Base.**

```
class Base:
    def function1(self):
        print("This function is in Base.")
```

Now we have a derived class inherited from Base class named as
Intermediate_1,

```
class Intermediate_1(Base):
    def function2(self):
        print("This function is in Intermediate_1 class")
```

Also another class **Intermediate_2** inherited from class Base,

```
class Intermediate_2(Base):
    def function3(self):
        print("This function is in Intermediate_2 class.")
```

Here, we see the multiple inheritance, a new class named **derived**
inherited from the two classes i-e **Intermediate_1** and **Intermediate_2**
as follows,

```
class Derived(Intermediate_1, Intermediate_2):
    def function4(self):
        print("This function is in derived class.")
```

Now we created a new instance **obj** for class **Derived**.

```
obj=Derived()
```

Also when we call functions from the classes we will get the following
outputs,

```
obj.function1()
obj.function2()
obj.function3()
obj.function4()
```

```
This function is in Base.
This function is in Intermediate_1 class
This function is in Intermediate_2 class.
This function is in derived class.
```

Task: Make a super class **Person()** and sub class **Empolyee ()**. The super class Person should have attributes in the constructor person_name and person_age. The sub class Employee also have new attribute ID.

14.5 Encapsulation

As the word says, it encloses something in it like a capsule. When we make any sub class then it can easily access every variable or method of super class. So if we want to keep it private?

For keeping them private we use the concept of encapsulation.

 **Knowledge:**

Encapsulation gives us security and flexibility. It hides the data of a class form direct illegal access.

We will see how to make

- Private variable
- Private method

To make a variable private we use two underscore before the variable name. In the following, we have a class name **Car**. Here the attribute **self.__engine** is the private attribute because we use underscore with it.

```
class Car:
    def __init__(self):
        self.make = "Corvette"
        self.model = "Stingray"
        self.__engine = "6.2L V-8"
    def get_description(self):
        return "The car is " + self.make + self.model
```

Now we define instance **Car_1** of class **Car()**.

```
Car_1 = Car()
```

Now we call the method **get_description** from the class **Car.** This method returning the attribute **self.make** and **self.car** from the class and prints the statement as follows,

```
print(Car_1.get_description())
```

```
The car is CorvetteStingray
```

We know that engine is the private attribute of the class **Car**. It means that we can't access it. If we try we get an error like the following

```
print(Car_1.__engine)
```

```
--------------------------------------------------------------------
----------
AttributeError                                Traceback (most recent c
all last)
<ipython-input-110-e81187306527> in <module>
----> 1 print(Car_1.__engine)

AttributeError: 'Car' object has no attribute '__engine'
```

Now we see that how we can make a method private. For that we again use two underscores (__) before the method name.

Again looking above example,

```
class Car:
    def __init__(self):
        self.make ="Corvette"
        self.model = "Stingray"
    def __engine(self):
        return "6.2L V-8"
    def get_description(self):
        return "The car is" +self.make + self.model
```

Here we define a method ***def__engine***(self) which is private because of using underscores with it.

Now we define instance ***Car_1*** of class ***Car()***

```
Car_1 = Car()
```

Again calling the method **get_description** from the class **Car**. This method returning the attribute **self.make** and **self.car** from the class and prints the statement as follows

```
print(Car_1.get_description())
```

```
The car is CorvetteStingray
```

Now if we call method **__engine** from the class **Car()**. Then we can't able to access and following error will generates,

```
print(Car_1.__engine())
```

```
-----------------------------------------------------------------
---------
AttributeError                          Traceback (most recent c
all last)
<ipython-input-118-2a95e6716951> in <module>
----> 1 print(Car_1.__engine())

AttributeError: 'Car' object has no attribute '__engine'
```

14.5.1 Accessing private members

Now if we want to access these private attribute or private method we can easily do. Recalling the above examples. We merged two above codes of private variable and private member.

Now this block of code consist of private attribute **self.__engine_name** as well as private method **def__ engine,**

```
class Car:
    def __init__(self):
        self.make ="Corvette"
        self.model = "Stingray"
        self.__engine_name = "6.2L V-8"
    def __engine(self):
        return "6.2L V-8"
    def get_description(self):
        return self.make + self.model + " is the car"
```

First define instance **Car_1** for class **Car()** as follows

```
Car_1 = Car()
```

Now first we access private attribute as follows,

```
print("Accessing Private variable: ", Car_1._Car__engine_name)
```

Accessing Private variable: 6.2L V-8

Now access private method as follows,

```
print("Accessing Private Method: ", Car_1._Car__engine())
```

Accessing Private Method: 6.2L V-8

Note that we use one underscore (_) before private attributename and private method name.

Great! We get all the private value.

14.6 Polymorphism

Polymorphism is a very important concept in programming. It is a Greek word. As **Poly** means many and **morphism** means forms so polymorphism means many forms. In python it means that we use same function name but the functions uses different signatures for different types.

Information: Its also allows us to use similar names of method in derived class as used in base class

The following methods are used for polymorphism:

- Polymorphism with functions and objects
- Polymorphism with Class Methods
- Polymorphism with Inheritance

We will see all these methods one by one.

14.6.1 Polymorphism with functions and objects

In this method of polymorphism, we can create a function that is able to take any kind of object.

Let's do an example related to Polymorphism using functions and objects. Here we a class *Car()*. In *Car()* we have three method defined *company()* , *model()* and *color()* as follows

```
class Car:
    def company(self):
        print("Car belongs to Honda company.")
    def model(self):
        print("The Model is Civic.")
    def color(self):
        print("The color is Blue.")
```

Also we have another class **Bike().** This class also have three methods having the same name as class **Car()** i-e **company(), model()** and **color()** as follows,

```
class Bike:
    def company(self):
        print("Bike belongs to Raleigh company.")
    def model(self):
        print("The Model is RRA.")
    def color(self):
        print("The color is black.")
```

Now we created a function called **func()** which will take an object named as obj. Now we call the methods **company(), model()** and **color()** each of which is defined in the above two classes i-e **Car()** and **Bike()**

```
def func(obj):
    obj.company()
    obj.model()
    obj.color()
```

In the following block, we created instances **car** and **bike** of the classes **Car()** and **Bike()**

```
car = Car()
bike = Bike()
```

Here we call both instances i-e *car* and *bike* which gives us the following output,

```
func(car)
func(bike)
```

```
Car belongs to Honda company.
The Model is Civic.
The color is Blue.
Bike belongs to Raleigh company.
The Model is RRA.
The color is black.
```

14.6.2 Polymorphism with Class Methods

In this method we will see that how python can use our different defined class types in similar way. In this method, first we create **for loop** that iterates though a tuple of objects. After that, we will call that method. As we assume that all these methods actually exists in each of the defined class.

Let's do an example,

Here we have class *Female()* having attributes *name* and *age.* Also we have three methods in it named as *info, welcome* and *goodbye*

```
class Female:
    def __init__(self, name, age):
        self.name = name
        self.age = age
    def info(self):
        print(f"I am a girl.My name is {self.name}.I am {self.age} years old.")
    def welcome(self):
        print("Hello")
    def goodbye(self):
        print("Good Day!")
```

We defined another class **Male()** having attributes **name** and **age**. Also the methods use in this class having same names as in class **Female()**

```
class Male:
    def __init__(self, name, age):
        self.name = name
        self.age = age
    def info(self):
        print(f"I am a boy.My name is {self.name}. I am {self.age} years old.")
    def welcome(self):
        print("Hi")
    def goodbye(self):
        print("Bye Bye!")
```

First we created instances **f1** and **m1** of classes **Female()** and **Male()**. Now we call the above two classes by passing values of attributes. Here string values **Maria** and **22** assigned to attribute **name** and **age** of class **Female()**. Similarly, **Adrian** and **18** assigned to attributes **name** and **age** of class **Male()**

```
f1 = Female("Maria",22)
m1 = Male("Adrian", 18)
```

Now we created **for loop** which will iterates through the tuple of instances i-e *f1* and *m1*. When for loop iterates it calls the methods of these classes i-e *info, welcome* and *goodbye*

This loop executed for both classes *Female()* and *Male()*. When we run the program, we get the following output

```
for humans in (f1,m1):
    humans.welcome()
    humans.info()
    humans.goodbye()
```

```
Hello
I am a girl.My name is Maria.I am 22 years old.
Good Day!
Hi
I am a boy.My name is Adrian. I am 18 years old.
Bye Bye!
```

It refers to the use of a single type entity (method, operator or object) to represent different types in different scenarios.

14.6.3 Polymorphism with Inheritance

In this method, we use methods name for derived class same as used for base class. Till now we learnt that the derived class inherited all the methods and attributes from the parent class. But here we see that we can also modify those methods.

14.6.3.1 Method Overriding

It means that if we want to redefine certain attribute or method in the child class specifically to fit the child class.

Let do an example of this method of inheritance. Here we have a derived class *Bird()*. In this class we have methods *intro()* and *flight()* as follows,

```python
class Bird:
  def intro(self):
    print("There are many types of birds.")
  def flight(self):
    print("Most of the birds can fly but some cannot.")
```

Now we have derived class *Crow* having only one method as follows,

```python
class Crow(Bird):
  def flight(self):
    print("Crow can fly.")
```

Following we have another derived class *Emu* also having only one method.

```python
class Emu(Bird):
  def flight(self):
    print("Emu cannot fly.")
```

Now we have defined instances of base class and derived classes. Instance *obj_bird* for class *Bird()*, *obj_cro* for class *Crow()* and *obj_emu* for class *Emu()*.

We can write the following code,

```
obj_bird = Bird()
obj_cro = Crow()
obj_em = Emu()
```

In this block of code we call different methods which will give us the following outputs,

```
obj_bird.intro() #Line 1
obj_bird.flight() #Line 2

obj_cro.intro() #Line 3
obj_cro.flight() #Line 4

obj_em.intro() #Line 5
obj_em.flight() #Line 6
```

```
There are many types of birds.
Most of the birds can fly but some cannot.
There are many types of birds.
Crow can fly.
There are many types of birds.
Emu cannot fly.
```

- As *obj_bird* is the instance of *Bird()* so in first two lines when we call method *intro* and *flight* of base class *Bird* then, it prints the respective statements.
- Note when we call the method *intro* of the derived classes *Crow()* (in line 3) and *Emu()* (in line 5) ,they used the methods from base class *Bird()* and prints the statement as

    There are many types of birds.

- But when we call the method *flight()* of derived classes *Crow()* (in line 4) and *Emu()* (in line 6) then they override the print message.
- The both classes prints their own print statement defined in the method *flight()* rather than printing the statement defined in the method of base class.

14.7 Overloading Operators

In python, we have a lot of overloading operators. Let do an example,

Here we have a class named it as *Vector()* as follows,

```
class Vector:
    def __init__(self, a, b):
        self.a = a
        self.b = b

    def __str__(self):
        return 'Vector (%d, %d)' % (self.a, self.b)

    def __add__(self,other):
        return Vector(self.a + other.a, self.b + other.b)
```

Note that we use ___add___ method in the class to add *vectors*

In the following block we pass the values representing the dimension of vectors and get the following output,

```
v1 = Vector(2,10)
v2 = Vector(5,-2)
print (v1 + v2)
```

```
Vector (7, 8)
```

Similarly, we have other overload operations in the following table,

Binary Operators	Methods	Assignment Operators	Methods
+	__add__(self, other)	+=	__iadd__(self, other)
-	__sub__(self, other)	-=	__isub__(self, other)
*	__mul__(self, other)	*=	__imul__(self, other)
/	__truediv__(self, other)	/=	__idiv__(self, other)
//	__floordiv__(self, other)	//=	__ifloordiv__(self, other)
%	__mod__(self, other)	%=	__imod__(self, other)
**	__pow__(self, other)	**=	__ipow__(self, other

Similarly, we have comparison and unary operators as follows,

Comparison Operators	Method	Unary Operators	Methods
<	__lt__(self, other)	-	__neg__(self, other)
>	__lt__(self, other)	+	__pos__(self, other)
<=	__lt__(self, other)	~	__invert__(self, other)
>=	__ge__(self, other)		
==	__eq__(self, other)		
!=	__ne__(self, other)		

> 💡 **Knowledge:** Over loading in programming means to define two or more **functions** with the same name and in the same scope.

In python we also have some overload method i-e

__init__ (self [,args...])

This is a constructor (with any optional arguments)

__del__(self)

This is destructor able to deletes an object

__repr__(self)

This able to evaluates string representation

__str__(self)

This able to print string representation

__cmp__ (self, x)

This is used for object comparison.

Chapter 15

Data Files

Till now, we covered all major topics of Python. We created variable, list, dictionaries, define the classes, work on loops etc.

But all the values generated during programming or execution of programs will disappeared after the program close. All these values, variables not stored permanently.

☀ **Information:** Like working on Microsoft word, Spreadsheet we have to save the file so that we can get it anytime we want.

Can we write all the values generated through code to the data file? So when our program closes we just go to that data file to read the text. In this chapter we see how to do this all.

We can read the data from the files and can also write data in the files.

15.1 Reading and Writing in external file from Python code

In python the file operation takes place in these following steps

- Open the file
- Read or write in the file
- Close the file

We can read and write files by using a function **with open()**.

Syntax:

with open("file_name.txt", "mode")as file:

This function needs the following two parameters,

- **File name**

  The name of file which we want to access.

- **Mode**

  In this parameter python decide that whether we have to read the data from file *file_name.txt* or have to write the data to the file *file_name.txt*. There are three basic modes,

  - Read
  - Write
  - Append

Note that the comma(,) followed by parameter **mode**

The **as** in the syntax is a keyword returns a handler to the file. Python needs a handle in order to get into the file. In this case, I've given it a handle named **file.** The line ends with the colon **(:)**

 Hint: We can write any name instead of file

15.1.1 Writing to text file

We have to write the writing mode as w

Syntax:

with open("my_file.txt", "w")as file:

file.write("This is my file")

Here we pass the file named **my_file.txt**. The line 2 starts with the name of file handle we specified in line 1, then a dot**(.)** followed by keyword **write()**. Inside the parenthesis we write string which we want to store in the file.

Important: For example, if the file not exists, then write mode will first create the file and then add text to it.

```
with open("new_file.txt","w")as file:
    file.write("Hello! Data Files.")
```

First this writing mode will create a file and named it as *new_file.txt* and write *Hello! Data Files.* in the file.

Also we can use this mode by storing a string in a variable. First we store string in the variable *intro* as follows,

```
intro="Hello! Data Files."
```

Then we pass the variable *intro* in the method *write,* as following,

```
with open("new_file.txt","w")as file:
    file.write(intro)
```

15.1.2 Reading from the text file

The reading mode is represented by **r**.

Syntax: We pass two parameters in the function **with open().** The line 2 starts with the name of a variable, then name of file handle *file*, then a dot(.) followed by keyword **read().**

with open("file_name.txt", "r")as file:

content =file.read()

The function *read()* will read all the data from the file named *my_file.txt* and saved to the variable *content,* then we print the variable *content* which shows all the data of the file.

> **Remember**: If the file doesn't exist then the read mode **"r"** will throw an error.

```
with open("new_file.txt","r")as file:
    content=file.read()
print(content)
```

Hello! Data Files.

Now we read the data from the file *new_file.txt* created above. This shows the text inside that file.

15.1.3 Writing in the append mode

Append mode is represented by "a".

Syntax:

with open("file_name.txt, "a")as file:

file.write("This text is written is append mode")

When we use the mode write **"w"** the function **with open** opens the file and write the text. When we get out of the body of function **with open()**, then the file will automatically close. Now if we have to write more text to same file then the previous text will disappeared and replaced by new text.

If we want previous as well new text in that file, then we will use append mode. As append mode allows us to write further.

```
with open("new_file.txt","a")as file:
    file.write("Now I am writing this text in append mode")
```

Here we don't want to remove the previous text and want to write more text to same file *new_file.txt.* Now we see that the new text don't over write the previous text "Hello! Data Files.*"* but we further add the text "Now I am writing this text in append mode".

```
with open("new_file.txt","r")as file:
    content=file.read()
print(content)
```

Hello! Data Files.Now I am writing this text in appending mode

We see that the text added to the *file new_file.txt*

We have further modes:

- w+
- r+
- a+

15.1.4 w+ mode

The w+ mode also allows us both to read the file as well as write the data in the file.

If the file not exists then w+ mode first create a file of that name then write the data to it.

Here we just created a new file named it as *new_file_1.* First the file will create and the text "In this mode we can read and read the text" added to that file, works same as **w** mode.

```
with open("new_file_1.txt","w+")as file:
    file.write("In this mode we can read and write the text.")
    print(file.read())
```

Note that, we print the function *file.read()* but nothing print. The reason is that the call *file.read()* will try to read from the end of the file and returns the empty string.

So we use the method **seek()**. This method sets the current position of the pointer at the offset. As we pass zero so it sets to index zero. We can write as follows,

```python
with open("new_file_1.txt","w+")as file:
    file.write("In this mode we can read and write the text.")
    file.seek(0)
    print(file.read())
```

In this mode we can read and write the text.

Great! We printed the text in the file

💡 **Knowledge:** We assume that the file should be in the same folder as the python program that opening it. But if the file is in the sub folders we have to give the file path instead of just giving the name of that file.

We use backward slash in windows as follows,

   With open("main_folder/file_name.txt", "mode")as file:

We use a forward slash on OS X and Linux as follows,

   with open("main_folder\file_name.txt", "mode")as file:

15.1.5 r+ mode

The r+ mode allows us both to read the file and write in the file.

In mode works for the existing files.

```
with open("new_file_1.txt","r+")as file:
    file.write("In this mode we can read and write the text.")
    file.write("But this will not create a file.")
    file.seek(0)
    print(file.read())
```

In this mode we can read and write the text.But this will not crea te a file.

Here we also use the method **seek()** to set the current position of the pointer at zero index.

Hint: We can see the current position of cursor by using a method **tell()**.This method returns the current position in number of bytes. We can use this method as follows,

```
with open("new_file_1.txt","w+")as file:
    file.write("In this mode we can read and write the text.")
    print(file.tell())
```

44

It means that now the cursor position is at the last of the following line,

In this mode we can read and write the text.

15.1.6 a+ mode

This mode opens a file for both appending and reading. The file pointer is at the end of the file if the file exists. The file opens in the append mode.

```
with open("new_file_1.txt","a+")as file:
    file.write("This text is written in a+ mode.")
    file.seek(0)
    print(file.read())
```

```
In this mode we can read and write the text.But this will not crea
te a file.This text is written in a+ mode.
```

In this mode, text is not over write but further added to the file like appending mode *a*

Remember: If the file does not exist, it creates a new file for reading and writing.

We have other modes in the following table

Modes	Description
x	Opens a file for exclusive creation. If the file already exists then this mode create an error.

t	Opens a file in text mode
b	Opens the file in binary mode
rb	Use for reading a binary file.
rb+	For reading or writing a binary file
wb	Opens a file for writing only in binary format. Overwrites the file if the file exists.
wb+	For writing a binary file
ab+	Opens a file for both appending and reading in binary format.

Task: Write a programme using all modes given in the above table one by one.

Chapter 16

Modules

In this chapter we will discuss that what actually modules are? Why we need it? Imagine that we have a file having a lot of variables, classes and function. This all will create a mess and we as a programmer get confused, so we stored these functions in a separate file called **Module.**

Module is same as code library. It helps us to logically organise our Python code. With the help of module,

- We group related code to module which make easier to understand and use.
- We write a function once and call it from other programs.
- We can use code written by other coders by writing their modules.

Syntax: We can give any name to the file we like. When we save the file we use extension **.py** with the name of the file.

my_file.py

16.1 Functions in module

In this section, we will discuss that how to create a module consist of functions and how we can use that module.

16.1.1 Creating a module

To create a module we just use extension *.py*. Let's do an example.

In the following block of code we defined a function *greeting*

```
def greeting(name):
    print("Hello, " + name)
```

We saved this text file and named it as **greet.py**

Let's create another module.

```
def add(a,b):
    return a+b
def sub(a,b):
    return a-b
def mul(a,b):
    return a*b
def div(a,b):
    return a/b
```

Here we defined four basic math operations. We save this text file named it **operations.py**

 Hint: We use the text file to create a module.

16.1.2 Use a module

Now we can use the module we created above by using keyword **import**.

First we open another code file then load the module by using the following syntax,

load.file_name.py

First we write load then a dot **(.)** followed by file name. Here we load the module named **greet.py** as follows,

```
%load greet.py
```

By running the above line, all the code loaded in the block as follows,

```
# %load greet.py
def greeting(name):
    print("Hello, " + name)
```

Hint: The hash sign will automatically appear at the start of line and make the first line as a comment.

Now we import the module which we loaded, by using the keyword
import

```
import greet
greet.greeting("Ainne")
```

```
Hello, Ainne
```

We called the greeting function by passing the string *Ainne*

Important: When we use function from the module we will use the following syntax,

module_name.function_name()

In the following, we load the module named **operations.py** which we
created above,

```
# %load operations.py
def add(a,b):
    return a+b
def sub(a,b):
    return a-b
def mul(a,b):
    return a*b
def div(a,b):
    return a/b
```

In the following block we import this module,

```
import operations as op
```

> **Hint:** The reason behind importing *operations as op* is actually
> we are shortening the phrase **"operations"** to **"op"** to make your code
> easier to read. We can use any word we want instead of **op.**

Now we can call any function in the module. In this module we have four
functions i-e *add(), sub(), mul()* and *div().*

In the following block we call the function **add** by passing the integer
values **2** and **3,** which gives us output by adding both values.

```
op.add(2,3)
```

5

Now we call function ***div()*** by passing integer values ***4*** and ***5***.This function will give us the output by dividing them i-e as ***4*** dividing by ***5*** equals to ***0.8***

```
op.div(4,5)
```

0.8

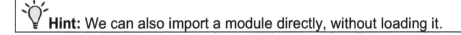

Hint: We can also import a module directly, without loading it.

16.2 Variables in module

The module can contain variables of all type for example,

- Array
- Object
- Dictionaries

16.2.1 Creating a module containing dictionary

Here we have a dictionary, named it ***info_of_person***.

```
info_of_person={"Name":"Hafsa","Age":"25","Country":"Canada"}
```

We create a module by saving this text file and we named the file as ***person1.py***.

16.2.2 Importing a module

Here we import module ***person1*** which we created above.

```
import person1
```

Now we can access any value of the dictionary *info_of_person* by passing the name of the key. In the following block of code, we pass the key *Name* and we get its string value *Hafsa* as an output,

```
a = person1.info_of_person["Name"]
print(a)
```

```
Hafsa
```

Also, we can get the string *Canada* by passing the key *Country,*

```
a = person1.info_of_person["Country"]
print(a)
```

```
Canada
```

16.3 Classes in module

In this, we will see that how we can import a class from another file.

16.3.1 Creating a module

Here we have a class *House()* having a method *description()* as following,

```
class House():
    def _init_(self,price,country):
        self.price = price
        self.country = country
    def description(self):
        print(f"The average price of houses located in {self.country} is {self.price}")
```

Now we save this text file and named it as ***estimate.py***

16.3.2 Use a module

We import the module ***estimate*** as follows,

```
import estimate
```

Now, we define instance *h* of the class *House()* by passing the values of arguments i-e ***price*** and ***country***

```
h=House("$286,067","England")
```

Now we call the method ***description()*** of the class *House()* for instance *h* as follows,

```
h.description()
```

```
The average price of houses located in England is $286,067
```

Great! We get the output by calling the class from other code file.

16.4 Import from the Module

Let's imagine that we have a module consists of a lot of classes, function, dictionaries and variables, but we just want to import any specific class from that module. In python we can choose to import only parts from a module, by using the keyword *from.*

Recalling the previous example, related module *estimate*. Here we can add another class *Bed()* as follows,

```python
class House():
    def __init__(self,price,country):
        self.price = price
        self.country = country
    def description(self):
        print(f"The average price of houses located in {self.country} is
{self.price}")
class Bed():
    def __init__(self,price):
        self.price = price
    def description(self):
        print(f"The average price of bed is {self.price}")
```

And save this file named it as *price.py*. Now we have to import *Bed()* from the module. So, we can write the following,

```python
from price import Bed
```

Here we define instance *b* for class *Bed()* by passing the value *$1000*

```python
b=Bed("$1000")
```

Now we call the method *description()* as follows,

```
b.description()
```

The average price of bed is $1000

In this way we can import anything from module

16.5 Built-in Modules

There are several build-in modules, which we can use whenever we want. For example in the following code we import build-in function *platform*

```
import platform
```

Now we have to specify that what we want to find out. If we want to know in which system we are running this code then we write as follows,

```
x = platform.system()
print(x)
```

Windows

Similarly, we can find the version of the python we are using, like the following,

```
x = platform.python_version()
print(x)
```

3.7.6

It shows that we have python version *3.7.6*

This will display a list consists of all available modules.

16.6 Built-in Function

We have a lot of build in functions in python. In the following example, we used build-in function *dir()*.

```
import math
x = dir(math)
print(x)
```

```
['__doc__', '__loader__', '__name__', '__package__', '__spec__', 'acos', 'acos
h', 'asin', 'asinh', 'atan', 'atan2', 'atanh', 'ceil', 'copysign', 'cos', 'cos
h', 'degrees', 'e', 'erf', 'erfc', 'exp', 'expm1', 'fabs', 'factorial', 'floo
r', 'fmod', 'frexp', 'fsum', 'gamma', 'gcd', 'hypot', 'inf', 'isclose', 'isfini
te', 'isinf', 'isnan', 'ldexp', 'lgamma', 'log', 'log10', 'log1p', 'log2', 'mod
f', 'nan', 'pi', 'pow', 'radians', 'remainder', 'sin', 'sinh', 'sqrt', 'tan',
'tanh', 'tau', 'trunc']
```

This will display all the function and variable names present in a module i-e **math**

Task: Use the build-in module **math.** From this module you have to print the value of **pi.**

Chapter 17

CSV Files

Like in the previous chapter, where we write the data through python code in the text file, we can also write data in CSV files.

CSV stands for **comma separated values.** It means that separator of each value is comma. We write comma after writing the first value then write the second value put a comma then write third value and so on.

> **Important:** A CSV contains only **text** in it.

CSV files are basically simplified version of the spreadsheet or database.

Here is the excel file,

Year	Club	Winner
2015	Barcelona	Lionel Messi
2016	Real Madrid	Cristiano Ronaldo
2017	Real Madrid	Cristiano Ronaldo
2018	Real Madrid	LokaModric
2019	Barcelona	Lionel Messi

Now we can import above excel file as a CSV file. So the CSV file looks like as follows,

Year, Club, Winner

2015, Barcelona, Lionel Messi

2016, Real Madrid, Cristiano Ronaldo

2017, Real Madrid, Cristiano Ronaldo

2018, Real Madrid, Loka Modric

2019, Barcelona, Lionel Messi

Hint: As the value of each cell becomes comma separated values and each row in spreadsheet becomes separate line in CSV file.

We can do the following three things in CSV files as we did in text files

- Read
- Write
- Append

17.1 Reading the CSV files

If a CSV file exists we can read the data from it easily.

Syntax: First we import **csv**, then open the file using function **with open()**. Also, we have to assign a file handle i-e **file**. With the help of this file handle, python will access the data of the CSV file. In line 3 we define a variable which equals to the function *csv.reader.*

import csv

with open(file_name.csv)as file:

variable = csv.reader(file)

Note that we pass the file handle *file* as an argument.

💡 **Important:** The data of the CSV files returned by the function *reader* will not in the useable form.

We use the following syntax to make the data useable.

with open("my_file") as file:

content = csv.reader(file)

content_of_competetion=[]

foreach_line in content:

content_of_competetion+=each_line

print(content_of_competetion)

We use *for* loop to extract all data lines in the form of list.

Here we created empty list *content_of_competition*. We are appending each line which is coming from CSV file *content* in the list *content_of_competition*

Let's do an example. We write the following data into text file and named it as **competition.csv**

```
Year,Club,Winner
2015,Barcelona,Lionel Messi
2016,Real Madrid,Cristiano Ronaldo
2017,Real Madrid,Cristiano Ronaldo
2018,Real Madrid,Loka Modric
2019,Barcelona,Lionel Messi
```

We first import **csv** as follows,

```
import csv
```

Now we open csv file ***competition.csv*** by using a function ***with open.*** Python will access the data of the CSV file with the help of file handle i-e ***file***. We define a variable ***content*** which equals to the function ***csv.reader()***. Now with the help of ***for loop,*** we extracted data and print it.

```
with open("competition.csv") as file:
    contents = csv.reader(file)
    for content in contents:
        print(content)
```

We run the above block of code which gives us the following output,

```
['Year', 'Club', 'Winner']
['2015', 'Barcelona', 'Lionel Messi']
['2016', 'Real Madrid', 'Cristiano Ronaldo']
['2017', 'Real Madrid', 'Cristiano Ronaldo']
['2018', 'Real Madrid', 'Loka Modric']
['2019', 'Barcelona', 'Lionel Messi']
```

> 💡 **Hint:** When we don't give any parameter of mode **(r,w)** to the CSV file by default it will read that file.

Note that the output data is in the form of multiple lists. So we merge all of data into single list by defining the empty list i-e *competition* as following,

```
import csv
with open("competition.csv") as file:
    contents = csv.reader(file)
    competition = []
    for content in contents:
        competition += content
print(competition)
```

By running this, we will get the output as follows

```
['Year', 'Club', 'Winner', '2015', 'Barcelona', 'Lio
nel Messi', '2016', 'Real Madrid', 'Cristiano Ronald
o', '2017', 'Real Madrid', 'Cristiano Ronaldo', '201
8', 'Real Madrid', 'Loka Modric', '2019', 'Barcelon
a', 'Lionel Messi']
```

Great!

Task:

Open any CSV file from your desktop to *read*. If there is no any file then first create csv file. Use spreadsheet software such as Microsoft Excel installed on your computer. Type some data in the cells and print them by using programme.

Hint:

- When you are ready to save your file, go to: File > Save As. In the file name field, use the drop-down menu to select "CSV - comma delimited.

- Before you start you must have to import csv and well as import pandas.

- You must have to pass the name of the file with its path i-e

    data =pandas.csv(r" file_path / file_name")

17.1.1 Picking information out of them

Python is able to pick some specific value from the given list. Recalling the above example in which we have a list *competition.* Now if we pass any index the python displays the value of that index. For example, by passing the index **3** in the list **competition** gives the value **2015**

```
print(competition[3])
```

2015

Similarly, by passing the index **10** in the competition give value **Real Madrid**

```
print(competition[10])
```

Real Madrid

Remember: List index always starts from **0**.

We can also get the index number of any value in the list competition as follows,

```
competition.index('Year')
```

0

Important: When we have multiple similar values then index returns the first index of that value which appear first in the list. For example, the string value **Real Madrid** comes in the list at index **7**, **10** and **13** but, it return first index i-e **7**.

```
competition.index("Real Madrid")
```

7

Let's do something useful by using the concept of index.

```python
club = input("Enter the name of a club:")
index_number_of_club =competition.index(club)
index_number_of_winner = index_number_of_club + 1
winner =competition[index_number_of_winner]
```

Enter the name of a club:

```

```

We give the input as the string value *Barcelona*.

```python
club = input("Enter the name of a club:")
index_number_of_club =competition.index(club)
index_number_of_winner = index_number_of_club + 1
winner =competition[index_number_of_winner]
```

Enter the name of a club:

```
Barcelona
```

- First, we defined the user input and stored it to the variable *club*.
- Then the index value of string i-e *Barcelona* stored in the variable *index_number_of_club.*
- We know that the name of player is stored next to the club name so we add *1* to the index of club name i-e *Index_number_of_club.*
- Now the python looks the value against the *index_number_of_winner* in the list competition and stored the name in the variable *winner.*

At last, we print this line of code, which gives us the following output,

```
print("The winner was " + winner)
```

```
Enter the name of a club:Barcelona
The winner was Lionel Messi
```

We can modify the above code so that the user can get name of **winner** by entering the **Year**. We can do this just by changing the increment value. i-e **2** .We can write the code as following,

```
year= input("Enter the year:")
index_number_of_year =competition.index(year)
index_number_of_winner = index_number_of_year + 2
winner =competition[index_number_of_winner]
print("The winner was " + winner)
```

```
Enter the year:
```
| 2017| ⨯ |

By entering the string value **2017** we get the following output

```
Enter the year:2017
The winner was Cristiano Ronaldo
```

Task: Here you have the student list with the positions they achieved,

['Harry', ' first', 'Peter', 'second', 'Hanna', 'third']

Write a programme that find the first name of the student by giving input as the positions. (Hint: You have to decrease the index value by 1 to get the name of the student)

17.2 Writing in the CSV files

We can load data to any csv file by defining the name of that csv file.

Remember:

- If we don't have any file of such name the file will generate automatically and after that, the data is loaded.
- If the file exists and some data is already in that file then writing mode will overwrite that data.

Syntax:

The syntax is almost same as for reading a CSV file. Just we pass parameter *w* (in quotation marks) for writing data in it. Also we have to define a file handle. We call the function **writer** in the csv module.

The parameter **newline** (used in the syntax) having the value **None** by default. It generates empty line between two rows. We can remove that line.

$$newline = \text{""}$$

For technical reasons, we can't write data directly to the CSV file. So we defined a variable, and give any legal name to it. Then, the variable connected by a dot to the keyword **writerow**. Each row is loaded into the handler as a list.

import csv

with open("my_file", "w", newline= "") as file:

variable_name=csv.writer(file, delimiter= ",")

variable_name.writerow(["Year", "champion", "top score"]

variable_name.writerow(["Year 1", "champion 1", "top score 1"])

variable_name.writerow(["Year 2", "champion 2", "top score 2"])

variable_name.writerow(["Year 3", "champion 3", "top score 3"])

Knowledge: The purpose of using delimiter is to separate two words. It can be anything like space, comma(,), dash(-), tab, semicolons(;), pipes(|), carets(^) or fullstop(.)

Let's do an example. We want to create a list of FIFA World Cup Records.

- First the file **com.csv** is created as the file of this name doesnot exists
- We name the variable **data_handler**
- Then we writes five rows using the function **writerow()**

```python
import csv
with open("competitions.csv", "w", newline= "") as file:
    data_handler = csv.writer(file)
    data_handler.writerow(["Year", "champion", "top score"])
    data_handler.writerow(["1998", "France", "Davor Suker"])
    data_handler.writerow(["2002", "Brazil", "Ronaldo"])
    data_handler.writerow(["2006", "Italy", "Miroslav Klose"])
    data_handler.writerow(["2010", "Spain", "David Villa"])
```

We can check the loaded data by opening the file ***competitions.csv***

```
Year,champion,top score
1998,France,Davor Suker
2002,Brazil,Ronaldo
2006,Italy,Miroslav Klose
2010,Spain,David Villa
```

```
Year,champion,top score

1998,France,Davor Suker

2002,Brazil,Ronaldo

2006,Italy,Miroslav Klose

2010,Spain,David Villa
```

17.3 Appending to CSV files

We can append more data to existing file without removing the previous data.

Syntax: We can use *a,* for appending data into file.

> *import csv*
>
> *with open("my_file", "a", newline= "") as file:*
>
>   *variable_name=csv.writer(file, delimiter= ",")*
>
>   *variable_name.writerow(["Year 4", "champion 4", "top score 4"])*
>
>   *variable_name.writerow(["Year 5", "champion 5", "top score 5"])*

Let's do an example. Recalling the previous example in which we created the file *competitions.csv*. Now we can append more data to that file by the following way,

```python
import csv
with open("competitions.csv", "a", newline= "") as file:
    data_handler = csv.writer(file,delimiter=",")
    data_handler.writerow(["2014", "Germany", "James Rodriguez"])
    data_handler.writerow(["2018", "France", "Harry Kane"])
```

```
Year,champion,top score
1998,France,Davor Suker
2002,Brazil,Ronaldo
2006,Italy,Miroslav Klose
2010,Spain,David Villa
2014,Germany,James Rodriguez
2018,France,Harry Kane
```

Great! The new rows appended in the same file.

Task: Suppose you have any CSV file in your desktop. Through python programming append more rows in the CSV file. Go to your file and verify by checking new rows which appears in your CSV file

Chapter 18

Jason files

In chapter 17, we deal CSV files. In this chapter, we will see another file format Jason.

Jason stands for **JavaScript Object Notation**. As name says that it is something related to JavaScript but python programmers can also use this.

Recalling some concept from chapter 15, where we discussed about writing the data in the text file as follows,

```
with open("text_file.txt", "w") as f:
  f.write("Hello.I am writing in the text file!")
```

We can read the data from the file *text.txt* as following,

```
with open("text_file.txt", "r") as f:
   text_of_file = f.read()
print(text_of_file)
```

```
Hello.I am writing in the text file!
```

Now, we want to add a list rather than a string so, we first define a list *number* and then we write in the text file using function *with open()* as follows,

```
number = ["1", "2", "3"]
with open("numbers.json", "w") as f:
  json.dump(number,f)
```

But it will create the following error.

TypeError: write() argument must be str, not list

We can't save a Python list in a text file. You can only save a text string in it. To save a list in a text file, we can use CSV file, but best way is to use JSON file.

18.1 Working with JSON

JSON file has functions same as CSV files. We can do the following in JSON file,

- Read the file
- Write in the file
- Append in the file

Syntax: First we have to import module json. Then with the help of function **with open** we open a file.

At last, we write a module name **json.** Then, comes a dot followed by the function **dump**. This function will takes two arguments i-e the list name and the file handle

import json

list_name = ["m1", "m2", "m3"]

with open("my_file.json", "w") as file:

json.dump(list_name, file)

Knowledge: We use this following syntax to change the object into json strings.

print(json.dumps(object))

We can convert the following types of Python objects

- dict
- list
- tuple
- string
- int
- float
- True
- False
- None

When we convert python objects, we get the following json equivalent,

Python	Json
dict	Object

list	Array
tuple	Array
string	String
int	Number
float	Number
True	true
False	false
None	null

For example, the following give us the output null.

print(json.dumps(None))

18.1.1 List to JSON file

Let's see how we can write data in it. First we import **json,**

```
import json
```

Here we have a list *Gases* containing three items as follows,

```
Gases = ["Oxygen", "Hydrogen", "Nitrogen"]
with open("gases.json", "w") as file:
    json.dump(Gases,file)
```

First the file *gases.json* created, in which the list *Gases* load.

If we open a file *gases.json* we see the following output,

```
["Oxygen", "Hydrogen", "Nitrogen"]
```

We can also save a dictionary in the file

18.1.2 Dictionary to JSON file

Here we have a dictionary *Grades.* In the following dictionary, subject names are the **keys** and marks are the **values** of dictionary.

```
Grades = {"Math":"91","Physics":"86","English":"84"}
```

Now we save the dictionary in the same way as follows,

```
with open("grades.json", "w") as file:
    json.dump(Grades,file)
```

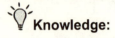

Knowledge:

The method *json.dump()* has following useful parameters,

- We can use indent parameter to define the numbers of indents. For example,

  $$json.dump(x , indent= 5)$$

- We can also change default value of separator as follows,

  $$json.dumps(x, indent=5, separators=(". ", " = "))$$

- If we want sort the result alphabetically, we can set True for parameter ***sort_keys*** as follows,

  $$json.dumps(x, indent=4, sort\_keys=True)$$

  In dictionary, this parameter will sort the result alphabetically by keys

Task

- Create a dictionary **person**. Write minimum three names as **keys** and **ages** as values of the dictionary

- Write the dictionary to a JSON file.

- Save the Python program to the Desktop and run it.

18.1.3 Accessing the information from JSON files

We can retrieve a **Python list** or **dictionary** from a **JSON file.** When we save the list or dictionary into JSON file we can read it easily.

Syntax: We again use the function ***with open*** and pass the file name as an argument. Then we call the function ***load()*** of the json module.

with open("my_file.json") as f:

my_file = json.load(f)

Recall the previous topic, in which first the file **gases.json** created. And then, the list **Gases** was loaded. Now if we want to retrieve information from the JSON file we write as follows,

```
with open("gases.json") as f:
    gases=json.load(f)
```

Now when we print **gases** it will give us the following output,

```
print(gases)
```

```
['Oxygen', 'Hydrogen', 'Nitrogen']
```

We also created a dictionary **grades.jason.** Now we retrieve the data of **grades.jason** as follows,

```
with open("grades.json") as f:
    grades=json.load(f)
```

By running this we get the following output.

```
print(grades)
```

```
{'Math': '91', 'Physics': '86', 'English': '84'}
```

Task:

1) Create a list of different countries name and assigned to the variable **list**. Save it in a JSON file. Then open the file and read it.

2) Open and read a JSON file containing any dictionary. Assign one of the values of the list to a variable. The key is a *string*.

(Hint: Don't indent the line that assigns the dictionary value)

Chapter 19

Exception

Syntax errors occur when compiler or interpreter caught errors during compile or interpret

Exceptions are run time errors. It means that nothing wrong in program but from the user side.

For example, developer writes a code which needs user defined input. Assume that the code is perfectly correct but, the user gives wrong input, which crash the whole code.

As a developer, we must keep in mind that if this scenario happens, what we must do something to protect the whole code.

Python manage the errors that arises during program execution by using special objects known as **Exceptions**

💡 **Hint:** Whenever the run time error occurs python is not sure what to do next, so it creates exception objects.

19.1 Handling errors

Errors/ Exception can be handle two keywords **try** and **except**

19.1.1 Try block

Programmers write main code in the try block.

19.1.2 Except block

Python executes the except block if things went wrong.

Syntax:

```
try:

    #body of try block

except:

    #body of except block
```

Knowledge: There may be more than one except block with one try block.

Syntax:

```
try:

    #body of try block

except:

    #body of except block

except:

    #body of except block
```

Let's suppose we have a following code, in which the python program asks about the file name from the user which will assign to variable **filename.** The **with open** function will open the file and function **read** will read the content and display it

```
filename = input("Enter the name of text file you want to read: ")
with open(filename) as f:
    print(f.read())
```

```
Enter the name of text file you want to read:
┌──────────────────────────────────────────┐
│                                          │
└──────────────────────────────────────────┘
```

To read the file, user must enter the file name.

```
filename = input("Enter the name of text file you want to read: ")
with open(filename) as f:
    print(f.read())
```

```
Enter the name of text file you want to read:
┌──────────────────────────────────────────┐
│ myfile                                   │
└──────────────────────────────────────────┘
```

The file **myfile** does not exists so it make the following error,

FileNotFoundError: [Errno 2] No such file or directory: 'myfile.txt'

If you code an exception, then this gives the user a clearer error message and also keeps the program from shutting down.

So, we can write it as the following block,

```
try:
    filename = input("Enter the name of text file you want to read: ")
    with open(filename) as f:
        print(f.read())
except FileNotFoundError:
    print("Sorry, " + filename + " not exists.")
```

As the *try* block says that take file from user then open it, after opening the file read the content in the file and also display it

The *except* block begins with the keyword except, followed by the keyword *FileNotFoundError* and a *colon*. When the except block run, the print statement inside its body will executed.

Now if we enter again the non-existing file i-e *myfile* then python display the following message,

```
Enter the name of text file you want to read: myfile
Sorry, myfile not exists.
```

Now, in the following example the python again need input from the user. First this code will display **Enter numerator**. After taking the value of numerator it asks for the denominator

Note that we converted both input values to integer by using *int,* as the type of input value is always string.

The exception block will print the reason of an error.

```
try:
    number1=int(input("Enter numerator:"))
    number2=int(input("Enter denominator:"))
    x=number1/number2
    print(x)
except Exception as e:
    print(f"An exception occured {e}")
```

Suppose if user enters the value *4* for the numerator and *2* for denominator than output will be,

```
Enter numerator:4
Enter denominator:2
2.0
```

Similarly, if user enters values *2* and *10* then the output will be as follows,

```
Enter numerator:2
Enter denominator:10
0.2
```

Great!

But, what happened when user enters the value **zero** for denominator?

```
Enter numerator:2
Enter denominator:0
An exception occured division by zero
```

It gives a clear message that error occurs due to the value zero for denominator and kept the whole program from dying.

19.1.3 Else Block

The function of keyword *else* is to define a block. This block will be executed if no error occurs.

Syntax:

```
try:

    #body of try block

except :

    #body of except block

else:

    #body of else block
```

```
try:
    print("Hello")
except:
    print("Something went wrong")
else:
    print("Nothing went wrong")
```

```
Hello
Nothing went wrong
```

Nothing wrong with the try block so else statement also executed. But if the error errors it will not run the else block as follows

```
try:
    x=3/0
    print(x)
except:
    print("Something went wrong")
else:
    print("Nothing went wrong")
```

Something went wrong

19.1.4 Finally Block

The keyword *finally* will also create a block. This block will be executed regardless the error occur or not by *try* block

Syntax:

try:

#body of try block

except :

#body of except block

finally:

#body of finally block

Like, here we are trying to open a file that is not writable,

```
try:
    f = open("greeating.txt")
    f.write("Hello")
except:
    print("Something went wrong when writing to the file")
finally:
    f.close()
```

19.2 Loop through JSON

If the user put wrong input then the programme will show error message. As, the programme should give another try to the user that he can enter another input. Recalling the previous example, in which user enter wrong value for the denominator. Now, he can enter another value for the denominator. For that we can use the **while loop** as follows,

Hint: The loop **while True** will keep repeating the statement until there is a **break** statement

```
while True:
    try:
        number1=int(input("Enter numerator:"))
        number2=int(input("Enter denominator:"))
        x=number1/number2
        print(x)
        break
    except Exception as e:
        print(f"An exception occured {e}")
```

As long as the user enters wrong value there is no break statement. Now, if user enters the value zero again for the denominator then the python will ask again for new values as following,

```
Enter numerator:2
Enter denominator:0
An exception occured division by zero

Enter numerator:
```


> 💡 **Hint**: The block of code that takes order is indented one level from the above line.

Task:

1) Write a code to open the file from your desktop, read and display the content of the file with the help of try-except block. Do this task using **while loop** to give the user another chance

   (**Hint:** End while loop with break statement)

2) Write the code beginning with the **while** statement. Try block will asks values of *a* and *b* from user. The *if statement* in try block will tests whether *a* divided by *b* has a remainder of *0*. If so, display a message "No reminder". Also make up the message for exception

   (**Hint:** Focus on the indentation level.)

19.3 Raise

The keyword *raise* is used to throw an exception. For example, we as a programmer can raise an exception if certain condition happened.

We have to define that what kind of error to raise

```
x=-5
if x < 0:
    raise Exception("Wite number greater than than zero")
```

```
--------------------------------------------------------------------------
Exception                                Traceback (most recent call last)
<ipython-input-3-197def847ccb> in <module>
      1 x=-5
      2 if x < 0:
----> 3     raise Exception("Wite number greater than than zero")

Exception: Wite number greater than than zero
```

Similarly, to raise **TypeError** we can write as follows,

```
x = "hello"
if not type(x) is int:
    raise TypeError("Only integers are allowed")
```

```
--------------------------------------------------------------------------
TypeError                                Traceback (most recent call last)
<ipython-input-4-d116f29775ec> in <module>
      1 x = "hello"
      2 if not type(x) is int:
----> 3     raise TypeError("Only integers are allowed")

TypeError: Only integers are allowed
```